George Russell (A.E.)

THE IRISH WRITERS SERIES
James F. Carens, General Editor

GEORGE RUSSELL (AE)	Richard M. Kain and James H. O'Brien
IRIS MURDOCH	Donna Gerstenberger
MARY LAVIN	Zack Bowen
FRANK O'CONNOR	James H. Matthews
ELIZABETH BOWEN	Edwin J. Kenney, Jr.
WILLIAM ALLINGHAM	Alan Warner
SEAMUS HEANEY	Robert Buttel
THOMAS DAVIS	Eileen Sullivan

GEORGE RUSSELL
(A.E.)

*Richard M. Kain
and James H. O'Brien*

Lewisburg
BUCKNELL UNIVERSITY PRESS
London: Associated University Presses

© 1976 by Associated University Presses, Inc.

Associated University Presses, Inc.
Cranbury, New Jersey 08512

Associated University Presses
108 New Bond Street
London W1Y OQX, England

Library of Congress Cataloging in Publication Data

Kain, Richard Morgan, 1908–
    George Russell (A. E.)

    (The Irish writers series)
    Bibliography: p.
    1. Russell, George William, 1867-1935. I. O'Brien,
James Howard, 1919–   joint author.
PR6035.U7Z69 1975   828'.8'09 [B]   72-3252
ISBN 0-8387-1101-4
ISBN 0-8387-1206-1 pbk.

Printed in the United States of America

Contents

7

Acknowledgments

Collaboration was suggested by Richard M. Kain, who knew of James O'Brien's thesis, "Theosophy and the Poetry of George Russell (A.E.), William Butler Yeats, and James Stephens," 1956. A division of responsibility was agreed upon, with the result that the first three biographical chapters are by Richard Kain, and the two dealing with theosophy and poetry by James O'Brien.

For permission to use material by A.E. under copyright, the authors wish to thank Mr. Diarmuid Russell of New York City and Mr. Alan Denson of Ellon, Scotland. The notation "D., Ms." in our text refers to the Denson Manuscript of letters by A.E. in the National Library of Ireland.

Mr. Kain wishes to thank the late Constantine Curran for sharing many memories of his former neighbor and friend, and the generous Dubliners whose contributions cannot be detailed. As ever, Louise Kain has proven to be at once constructive and cooperative.

Mr. O'Brien wishes to thank the following people for help in completing this study: Mr. Frank Gegenheimer, editor of *Arizona Quarterly*, for permission to use parts of Mr. O'Brien's article "A.E. and the Self," Autumn

1966; Henry Summerfield of the University of Victoria, whose biography of A.E. he read in manuscript; Monk Gibbon, Dublin, for permission to use Mr. Gibbon's thesis on A.E. in Trinity College, Dublin; and the Bureau for Faculty Research, Western Washington State College, for assistance in travel and typing. Mr. O'Brien is especially indebted to his wife, Patricia, for sustained encouragement and seemingly endless proofreading, and to Louise and Richard Kain, whose hospitality transformed the task of revising the manuscript into an enjoyable visit.

Chronology

1867	Born April 10, in Lurgan, County Armagh. Parents: Thomas Elias Russell and Marianne Russell.
1871	Attends Model School, Lurgan.
1878	Family moves to Dublin.
1880	Attends Metropolitan School of Art.
1882-1884	Attends Rathmines School.
1883-1885	Attends evening classes at Metropolitan School of Art.
1885-1888	Attends art classes at Royal Hibernian Academy.
1888 or 1889	Joins Theosophical Society, Dublin Lodge.
1890-1897	Works at Pim Bros., drapers, Dublin.
1891-1897	Lives at Theosophical Household, 3 Upper Ely Place.
1897	Begins work for Irish Agricultural Organization Society under Sir Horace Plunkett.
1898	Marries Violet North, June 9.
1902	First performance of his play *Deirdre*, April 2.

1902	Irish National Dramatic Society formed in February. Yeats, president; A.E., vice-president. A.E. resigns soon afterwards.
1904	August exhibition of paintings by A.E. and Count Markiewicz.
1904	Dublin Lodge of Theosophical Society revived in October.
1905-1923	Edits *The Irish Homestead.*
1923-1930	Edits *The Irish Statesman.*
1928	Lectures in the United States to raise money for *The Irish Statesman.*
1928	Receives Honorary degree from Yale University.
1928	Case against *The Irish Statesman* dismissed in November but the journal owes lawyers' fees of 2,500 pounds.
1929	Receives honorary degree from Trinity College, Dublin.
1930	Travels in America to raise money for Mrs. Russell's medical fees.
1932	Violet Russell dies, February 3.
1934-1935	American tour under auspices of the Department of Agriculture, December to March.
1935	Dies at Bournemouth, England, July 17.

George Russell (A.E.)

1

The Personality

As poet, painter, philosopher, George William Russell was the luminous center of the Irish Revival. The story of his well-known pseudonym illustrates his mysticism. One of his own visionary paintings haunted him; he heard a whispered "Aeon." Not knowing its meaning, he found the word soon thereafter on an open page in the National Library, and learned that it was a Gnostic term for the first created beings. He used it on a manuscript, and a compositor queried, "AE–?" Here was the occult symbol he needed.

Simone Téry's *L'ile des bardes* (1925) portrays the universal pundit:

> Have you doubts regarding Providence, the origin of the universe and its end? Go see A.E.–Are you seeking information on Gaelic literature, the Celtic soul, Irish history? Go see A.E.-Are you interested in painting? Go see A.E.–Do you want to know the exports of eggs. . .or how best to cultivate bees? Go see A.E.–Do you find society badly run, and want to better it? Run to A.E.'s. . . .You doubt yourself? Find life insipid? A.E. will give you confidence, will comfort you.–Do you need a friend? A.E. is always there. [trans. R. M. Kain]

Russell's Sunday evening is an unforgettable part of her essay. From the tram stop along dimly lighted streets and through the tiny front garden she wends her way. Within she hears the voices of writers, artists, and others gathered about the fire. It is like a large family, she feels, with A.E. the father. Indeed, with his benevolent smile, his friendly but piercing eyes, and his bearded face surrounded by a halo of smoke, he even resembles God the Father. Without dominating the conversation, he enlivens each guest, animating the poetry in the philosopher, the political economy in the poet. One thinks of Mrs. Ramsay in Virginia Woolf's *To the Lighthouse,* as he is described playing upon his friends "like a virtuoso."

A.E. comes to life in the pages of Joyce's *Ulysses.* His occultism, his belief in the anima mundi, his hospitality, his beard, bicycle and watch—all are there, and with more than a trace of absurdity. Still, Stephen Dedalus could rightly pun, "A.E.I.O.U." Joyce's debt was indeed both literary and financial, for A.E. had published three of the *Dubliners* stories in *The Irish Homestead* in 1904.

Joyce's attitude lies somewhere between the guarded criticism of Yeats and the unexpected reverence of George Moore. Yeats and A.E. were rivals and friends in the early days, differing on literary aims. In a famous letter of 1904 Yeats apologized to A.E. for some slighting remark by Lady Gregory which "I was foolish enough to quote." Yeats's rejection of sentimentality is famous: "Let us have no emotions, however abstract, in which there is not an athletic joy."

Apology was followed by analysis. In his autobiographical *The Trembling of the Veil* (1922) Yeats undertook the ungracious task of finding the sources of failure among his own generation in London and in Ireland. A.E.'s faults and virtues intermingle, for though he often "seemed incapable of coherent thought, and perhaps was so at certain moments," yet "I used to listen to him at that time, mostly walking through the streets at night, for the sake of some stray sentence, beautiful and profound." Good will made him uncritical, "turning cat to griffin, goose to swan." Perhaps it is the unfortunate influence of Emerson and Whitman, "writers who have begun to seem superficial precisely because they lack the Vision of Evil." The result is often "moral or poetical commonplace."

George Moore's long-rumored reminiscences worried all literary Dublin, including A.E., but when the first volume, *Ave,* appeared in 1911 A.E. was hero, the Church villain, and Yeats, with many others, somewhere between. On first reading A.E.'s poetry and prose, Moore exclaimed:

> It was just as if somebody had suddenly put his hand in mine, and led me away into a young world which I recognised at once as the fabled Arcady.

"Here is the mind of Corot," he reflected, "the happiness of immemorial moments under blossoming boughs." Evocative impressionism this, but it evokes the pagan, decadent spirit of the nineties rather than A.E.'s pantheistic solemnity. Only once does Moore's mischief creep in, when he asks how the Irish gods could have communicated with a mystic who knew no Irish. A.E.'s reply shows his characteristic combination of the practical and visionary:

'The Gods,' he answered, 'speak not in any mortal language; one becomes aware of their immortal Presences.'

In his second volume, *Salve* (1912), Moore recalls A.E.'s daily visits to "walk together to the great apple tree and sit there talking of Manet and the immortality of the soul." With the eye of a painter Moore describes a holiday on bicycles, visiting the prehistoric mounds of Dowth and Newgrange in the valley of the Boyne. He captures the sunny stillness of those summer days, the ever-changing tones in the sky and the waves of green below as A.E. discoursed on Druid mysteries. Encountering a farm girl, not an Arcadian shepherdess but a colleen driving cattle, A.E. remarked, "Before the tumuli, she was." A poem in five words. There was an "extraordinary evening" at an inn, when A.E. captivated guests with his conversation: "A. E. had ascended the mountain of the spirit and a Divine light was about him." The biblical echoes of this episode—the ascent of the mountain, the night at the inn—sound again in Moore's description of A.E. at a meeting of the Theosophical Society in Dawson Street:

He was sitting at a bare table, teaching, and his disciples sat on chairs, circlewise, listening. There was a lamp on the table, and it lit up his ardent, earnest face.

In Moore's final volume of *Hail and Farewell, Vale* (1914), the analogy with Christ is made explicit: "A.E.'s life is in his ideas as much as Christ's." Moore leaves Ireland thinking "of the friends he had left behind him—A.E. and the rest."

With this tribute W. M. Clyde concludes his account of 1935:

It may be that posterity, looking back on this present period of our poetry, will sum it up in those same words—"A.E. and the rest."

The opinion was not unanimous. As long ago as 1898 there were those who were not impressed. The Reverend Stopford Brooke made a diary entry, quoted in Rolleston's *Portrait of an Irishman* (1939):

George Russell, the Irish poet, came in to dine. And he talked—opalescently. George Russell has more stuff in him than Lionel Johnson, but he talked very sad stuff about his spiritualistic experiences, his visions, dreams, and phantasms. Everything he saw was either opalescent or irridescent, and I wished at times he would opalescence [*sic*] himself into an irridescent vision.

To Sean O'Casey A.E. was "Dublin's Glittering Guy," but the author is so obviously biased as to provide his own corrective. More telling is the observation by Desmond MacCarthy, quoted by O'Casey:

As years went on, fewer young men and women came of an evening to drink at A.E.'s fountain. When I inquired. . .I was told—A.E.? I haven't seen him. Nobody goes there now.

Yet even the cold light of today has not entirely obliterated the glow. Frank O'Connor, in *My Father's Son* (1968), admits that "He was a creature of habit, and his conversation, like his life, like his pictures, ran in patterns." He was, however, "a man of intense intellectual vitality." Perhaps the last word should be that of A.E.'s protégé, James Stephens, who said in 1948 that "he inclined to sit on the top of the morning all day."

2

Early Success

We first encounter Russell in art school in Dublin, where he met Yeats, the sculptor Oliver Sheppard, and the theosophist Charles Johnston. The time was about 1885; Yeats was twenty, Russell two years younger. Yeats recalled in *Reveries Over Childhood and Youth* (1914) that "he did not paint the model. . .for some other image rose always before his eyes." Though Russell gave up formal training he never ceased to sketch and paint, creating landscapes real or imaginary, as well as portraits, always with astonishing rapidity.

There was always a twinkle in the eye, too. John Eglinton's *Memoir* (1937) records his testimony before a Royal Commission in which he described four visiting academicians. One "was an excellent landscape painter," a second "painted bulls and cows," a third "cats and dogs," and the last "did not paint at all." Fortunately, "They never put their fingers on the students' work, which was probably the best thing they could have done."

From 1887 to 1897 Russell was active as theosophist

and poet, unusual for a drapery assistant. Eglinton's
brother, H. M. Magee, recalled that in the theosophical
Household where the adepts lived, A.E. always elicited
each member's "nobler qualities." In 1894 appeared:

HOMEWARD *
SONGS BY ***
THE WAY. A.E.

The ambiguous title suggests both "Homeward," and
"Homeward Songs." It is often transcribed with a colon
after "Homeward," but A.E. used a comma. He explained that it meant the soul's path toward its divine
source. Three years later *The Earth Breath and Other
Poems* was published.

The enthusiasm of the time is found in a letter from
A.E. to Yeats: "The gods have returned to Erin and
have centred themselves in the sacred mountains." He
predicts that with an awakening of "the magical
instinct" a new spirit is at hand: "Out of Ireland will
arise a light to transform many ages and peoples." The
Messianic dream was a golden thread in Irish culture.

A.E. was once as celebrated for his painting as for any
of his other work. Most characteristic is the dream
landscape, enshrouded by mist or twilight, in which
ethereal figures dance. Paul, in *The Avatars* (1933) is a
self-portrait, "painting the earth visible and invisible, all
the shapes the soul takes in its travels from earth to
sky." As he paints, "He could see swirling draperies,
flushed faces, loosened and rippling hair, the glint of a
white arm, a gleaming neck, the dance of lovely feet, all
sun-flecked, dazzling and bewildering as the anarchy of
flame and darkness in which they rioted." To John

Quinn A.E. wrote: "What I want to do is to paint landscape as if it had no other existence than as an imagination of the Divine Mind, to paint man as if his life overflowed into that imagination, and to paint the Sidhe as mingling with his life; indeed the unity of God and man and nature in one single being—an almost impossible idea to convey in paint."

He worked in various media. Among his watercolors is a series on the history of man's soul. He often sketched landscapes with colored chalk, and he also worked in pastels. He painted several murals in Dublin, two of which remain in fragmentary condition, those at the Household on Ely Place and those at the office of the *Irish Homestead,* recently described by James White in *The Arts in Ireland* (I, 3). Cosmic figures are clear—serpents, the lotus, streams of light, symbolic goddesses.

He also experimented in color prints and tapestry designs, the latter for Lily Yeats, as he reported to Yeats in mischievous mood: "I have been trying with great pleasure to turn a woman of the Sidhe into a Virgin for your sister to embroider." He adds that "I would dearly love to make a faery chapel and put mystical figures so that the good catholics who went there would become worshippers of the Sidhe without knowing it."

Striving toward the ecstatic led him into the arty style of the nineties. However highly his work had been applauded in his annual exhibitions from 1904 to 1915, the works are now faded, both literally and artistically, though Mr. White suggests that when the murals from the *Homestead* office are restored, "he will merit consideration as a most important and interesting symbolist artist of the period 1890-1920."

His earlier fame is represented by Joseph Holloway's diary entry on the exhibition of 1904, when A.E.'s work appeared with that of Constance Gore-Booth and the man she married, Casimir Dunin-Markievicz:

> The strange, misty, almost uncanny quality of all George Russell's work fascinated me to the extent of ignoring the work of the other two artists. If ever the Celtic Spirit of dreaminess and longing for something that is neither land nor sea was transplanted onto canvas, here that longing and dreaminess surely was. (September 3, 1904)

Katharine Tynan recalled lunching with A.E. at Sir Horace Plunkett's home at Foxrock (later burned by the Irregulars in the Civil War):

> I can remember his mild beam at me across the table against the background of his own beautiful paintings—to my purblind eyes a soft blur of all the lilacs and violets melting into dove-colour and silver,—which hang round the dining-room at Kilteragh.

The landscapes and portrait sketches were better. As the reviewer "B.P.F." said, "When he made painting the instrument of his inner illumination the result is generally bad and unpainterly: When he really looked at something the result was sometimes excellent." He had a clear eye for landscape, and some of his most effective drawing was done in crayon and ink, sketched on the spur of the moment when autographing his books. I own two examples, a copy of *Voices of the Stones* (1925)—two ranges of hills rising in the distance against a clear sky with one white cloud, a rocky hillside and the edge of a lake in the foreground—and a *Collected*

Poems (1931)—a craggy abutment with a luminous sky beyond. Others which I have seen are similar in subject and technique, the main outlines in ink, the forms covered by rapidly drawn crayon cross-hatching.

A.E.'s work is not easily available in reproduction, and thus a few citations may be helpful. Alan Denson's bibliography includes two early drawings, an 1885 profile of Oliver Sheppard the sculptor, done when they were fellow students, and a half-length sketch of Charles Weekes (a good likeness, as a contemporary photograph of the sitter indicates). Denson lists almost fifty portraits, two of which are to be found in standard books. An oil painting of Lady Gregory is reproduced in *Ireland's Abbey Theatre* (1952); its suggestion of both serenity and strength seems true to the personality. C. H. Rolleston's *Portrait of an Irishman* (1931), a memoir of his father, T. W. Rolleston, contains a 1901 photograph of A.E. painting a self-portrait. Denson's edition of the letters has a black and white reproduction of a letterhead in watercolor, approximately summer 1886, with a tree and two floating female figures. "The Potato Gatherers," peasant women leaning toward each other to lift a basket, is reproduced in Bruce Arnold's *A Concise History of Irish Art* (1968). The boldness of the figures against a brilliant sunset sky is softened by the merging of their lower limbs into the earth, which is emphasized by the sloping horizon line. The painting seems to symbolize the close relationship of humanity to the earth. Before we dismiss A.E.'s painting entirely as the spontaneous dabbling of an amateur we must notice the strong resemblance between "The Potato Gatherers" and the seething vitality of the later Jack Yeats, so much admired today.

A.E.'s painting, like most of his work, suffered from facility and immateriality. It seems destined to oblivion; there is no mention of his art in the *Encyclopaedia of Ireland* (1968). Yet for the first years of the century the work of this man pictured the unworldly side of the Irish Revival, just as the bold woodcuts of Jack Yeats captured the peasant, fisherman, villager, or vagabond of the Irish village. Austin Clarke, late dean of Irish poets, recalls in *A Penny in the Clouds* (1968) the impression made upon him by the work of A.E.:

> Every summer, A.E. stayed for a month in a hillside cottage...spending his days in reverie or in painting pictures. Sometimes, he went with his brushes and box of paints to the cliff-house, above Marble Strand where his friend, Hugh Law, lived...He had a remarkable power of visualization and when he returned to Dublin, he spent the week-ends at his easel, dipping his brushes into memory. I was fascinated by the unearthly hues of those landscapes, in which the May moon, pale as primrose, shone above the foam-edges along the strand where the vague forms of young girls could be seen.
>
> > A glimmer of dancing shadows
> > A dovelike flutter of hands.

The lines are from "Frolic," in *The Divine Vision* (1904). The last stanza reads:

> The whole of the world was merry,
> One joy from the vale to the height,
> Where the blue woods of twilight encircled
> The lovely lawns of the light.

The Celtic dream, perhaps more myth than reality, answered a deep-seated need for Ireland. In A.E.'s editorial, "The Nation and Beauty," the author urges that "A nation exists primarily because of its own imagination of itself." The search for a distinctive national spirit dated from the nineteenth century. Its own parliament abolished by the Act of Union in 1800, Ireland had sunk into stagnation. The native language was dying, and the Famine of the forties caused a drastic loss of population as well as unprecedented misery. The Irish were caricatured as boorish clowns, ignorant and violent.

When A.E. read the romantic histories of O'Grady his reaction was that of one "who suddenly feels ancient memories rushing at him, and knows he was born in a royal house." "It was the memory of race which rose up within me." Indeed, his career, like that of Yeats, provides an almost perfect model of the modern Irish experience of rising hope and ultimate disappointment. It was to have been a glorious spiritual quest, compounded of national pride and poetic imaginings.

Without practical activities to occupy them, both poets might have succumbed to despair. In A.E.'s case it was a most unlikely assignment. In 1897 he joined the staff of the Irish Agricultural Organisation Society (I.A.O.S.), founded by Horace Plunkett to develop rural cooperatives. Yeats was astonished at A.E.'s success "before he had even read a book upon economics or finance," and his ability "within a few months to give evidence before a Royal Commission. . .as an acknowledged expert, though he had brought to it nothing but his impassioned versatility."

Russell praised Plunkett in a letter of December 1901. He wrote Katharine Tynan Hinkson:

The average M.P. spends his holiday yachting but Plunkett

went through Connemara, Achill Enis and part of Donegal
with me day after day speaking to the farmers, going into
their houses, trying to inspire them with the idea of self
help and of cooperating.

"I never knew a man so unwearied in helping others,"
he concluded, words which could apply equally to A.E.
himself. Plunkett, characterized by Eglinton as "half
dreamer, half man born to be king," had found in
Russell a diligent worker and a voice for his dream.
"A.E.'s journalism," Eglinton wrote, "rose like a song
out of the bitter newspaper press of Ireland, building up
Plunkett's ideal kingdom." The appearance of a prophet
in what Joyce's Stephen Dedalus dismissed as "The pigs'
paper" must have been astonishing.

Astonishing, too, the influence. Henry Wallace recalled how A.E.'s *Irish Homestead* was read aloud in
Iowa; an article on A.E. was published in *Wallace's
Farmer,* August 15, 1913. Alan Denson's extensive
bibliography cites this item along with more than three
hundred books and articles containing allusions to A.E.
India, Germany, Italy, France, as well as the English-
speaking world are represented. An unexpected appearance of A.E.'s work is in the Department of Economics
at the University of Wisconsin. The Irish library and a
few paintings by A.E., Nathaniel Hone, and Jack Yeats
were assembled as an outgrowth of a study of land
problems in Ireland carried out in the summer of 1913
by a Professor Ely of the department.

A.E.'s authority was soon to diminish, however. John
Eglinton quotes an anecdote from Mrs. McCraith
Blakeney dating from a few weeks before the Easter
Rising. Susan Mitchell, A.E.'s close friend and assistant,
was already aware that his star was waning:

I said to Susan Mitchell as we left him, "Does he know how great his influence is?" "But is it?" she said sadly. "But he *is* great!" "Not in Ireland today," she murmured, with a sad little waft of vision.

Earlier, the poet-economist had had his doubts as to the effects of progress on rural Ireland. Only half-seriously he wrote a fellow committee member, the publisher T.P. Gill:

It was sacrilege to talk about banks as I did below Nephin, which is largely stocked with gods, immortals and fairies. I am sure they felt civilisation was threatening them and fought vainly against it.

An odd instance of conservation this, ecological protest from the fairy world! Russell continued, in whimsical vein:

I talked largely after the modern fashion about percentages, while the ancients of the skies pelted me with sleet. I was muffled up in two overcoats and defied the gods. I thought the gods would make a better fight and I have a half-disappointed feeling, for I believe we will have a bank.

Meanwhile Russell married an Englishwoman who had been active in Theosophy, a member of the Ely Place community. We hear and read little about Violet North, who married him in 1898. They had two surviving sons, Brian and Diarmuid. Frank O'Connor, who knew A.E. only in later life, reported that he never talked about his wife, and that though he "was extraordiniarily inquisitive about women...I had the feeling that he was unhappy in his marriage." John Eglinton, however, described the marriage as "a fortunate one," in that "She shared in all his beliefs," but the biographer admitted that "Russell could hardly be called a domestic man, and he always seemed as much disengaged from family ties as Socrates."

Perhaps A.E.'s genius was for friendship rather than for domestic attachment. His delight in discovering new talent became almost a standard Dublin joke. The singing birds he envisioned were variously termed his canaries or his poultry. As Yeats wrote to Katharine Tynan in 1906, the younger generation "show some increase of culture" in Ireland, but "nearly all their faults rise out of the newness of that culture," since "They are vague, self-conscious, literary," but "have not however yet learnt how to work at a poem." He pointed out that Russell's religious impulse led him to consider all souls equal though "They are never equal in the eyes of any craft." Here speaks the uncompromising technician, seldom satisfied even with his own magnificent poems.

Though some swans turned out to be geese, A.E. was responsible for discovering or at least encouraging the early work of Padraic Colum, Seumas O'Sullivan, James Stephens, and others. He writes to the American publisher, Thomas Mosher, in 1903, "I am also making a selection from lyrics written by young poets who are friends of mine here some of which I think are beautiful and all interesting." *New Songs* included lyrics by Colum, Starkey (Seumas O'Sullivan), Alice Milligan, Eva Gore-Booth, Thomas Keohler, Susan Mitchell, George Roberts, and Ella Young. Three editions of five hundred copies each appeared in 1904 and 1905. A.E.'s one-page preface voices his love of the poetry and his joy in publishing it:

I have thought these verses deserved a better fate than to be

read by one or two, not only on account of the beauty of
much of the poetry, but because it revealed a new mood in
Irish verse.

That is, a different mode than that of the patriotic
writers of *The Nation,* fifty years before. Shortly
afterward he was ecstatic over another find: "I have
discovered a new young poet. . .James Stephens who has
a real original note in him." So he wrote Katharine
Tynan Hinkson in December 1908, concluding that
"The greatest pleasure I find in life is discovering new
young poets."

In the emerging theater A.E. characteristically played
an important but often overlooked role. During its first
three years, from 1899 through 1901, the Irish Literary
Theatre had barely survived. The turning point came
when A.E. wrote, in one night, two scenes of a play
about Deirdre which were published by Standish
O'Grady in his *All-Ireland Review,* July 6, 13, and 20,
1901. The Fay brothers, one a typist, the other a clerk,
who had produced farces locally, urged A.E. to complete the play and let them perform it. It was, in the
words of Peter Kavanagh *(The Story of the Abbey
Theatre,* 1950), "the spark which really set the Irish
dramatic movement alight," for the production marked
"the real beginning of the Irish National Theatre—Irish
plays acted by Irish players in an Irish hall."

Maud Gonne's nationalistic group, Inghinidhe na
h-Eireann (Daughters of Ireland) performed A.E.'s
Deirdre and Yeats's *Kathleen ni Houlihan* on April 2, 3,
and 4, 1902. Despite the unsatisfactory room in which a
thin partition divided the "theatre" from a billiard hall,
the plays were well received. Joseph Holloway wrote in

his diary that "were it not for the unceasing distracting noises" the evening would have been a delight. The dazzling Maud Gonne gave a striking personification of Kathleen, and Maire Quinn played Deirdre. Maire Nic Shiubhlaigh (Mary Walker), the first actress to use an Irish name, recalls in *The Splendid Years* (1955) that A.E.'s rendition of the Irish heroine was appropriately mystical:

> *Deirdre* was presented under a gauze upon which Fay played a green arc, giving the stage a ghostly mist-like appearance. Costumes, made from designs by A.E., blended perfectly into the sombre background. The characters had the appearance of figures rising out of a mist.

Among others in the cast of this double bill were the Fay brothers, Dudley Digges, and the writers Padraic Colum and James Cousins. *The Freeman's Journal* interpreted A.E.'s rendition of Irish legend in terms which recall his exuberance at reading Standish O'Grady:

> It is evident that to A.E. the heroic past of Ireland is no mere storehouse of romantic legends, more or less authentic; for him, that past is a living reality and a source of spiritual inspiration. The old gods and heroes are, for A.E., the embodiment of everlasting forces. . .his figures move with a dignity and a beauty which accord well with our ideals.

Irish individualism has so often led to friction that the history of the Revival can easily become a story of feuds: Moore against Yeats, Yeats against A.E., O'Casey against Yeats. One after another, directors, writers, and actors were to leave the theatre society, disagreeing on

various matters of policy. The story has often been
glossed over, but it can be found at its fullest in Peter
Kavanagh's *The Abbey Theatre.* A.E., already the victim
of Standish O'Grady's attack on the staging of Irish
legend, was soon to be cast aside by Yeats. Russell had
been elected one of three vice-presidents of the Irish
National Society, formed in 1902. Attacks upon Synge's
early plays as insulting to Irish character led to the
resignations of the other two vice-presidents, Maud
Gonne in October 1903, and Douglas Hyde in March
1904. Shortly thereafter, A.E. resigned. Yeats wrote to
Quinn, "If all goes well, Synge and Lady Gregory and I
will have everything in our hands."

Between 1901 and 1905 A.E. also served on the
Publication Committee of the Irish Literary Society
(1901-1904), sponsored a Rural Library Association,
supported Hugh Lane in his efforts to purchase modern
French paintings for a municipal art gallery, and became
a charter member of the "Second Dublin Lodge" of the
Theosophical Society, in addition to publishing volumes
of prose and verse and carrying on the work of the
I.O.A.S. There would seem to have been little opportun-
ity to have involved himself in the theater, yet Maire Nic
Shiubhlaigh records that "For most of us during these
years, A.E. was the real leader of our movement,"
despite his casualness:

> he might have appeared just another, not very prepos-
> sessing, member of the little society, a bulky figure, sitting
> well out of the chatter, and the noise, puffing a pensive
> pipe. But his readiness to help on all occasions, his intense
> nationalism, the work he was always doing to further the
> interests of Ireland, both artistically and economically,
> made him, for me, the central prop of our whole

movement. . .He worked quietly, without any attempt to gain individual distinction.

Since Sean O'Casey's most cruel gibes are directed at A.E.'s love of adulation, the testimony of this actress is of some value. A.E. himself disavowed literary ambitions in his letter to his first publisher, Charles Weekes, written in the spring of 1907:

> My dear Honey, don't worry about me "coming along," I will never please you for between ourselves literature does not interest me enough to make me anxious to work hard at it. I simply want to live a natural energetic life and if a poem ever takes me along the way I will welcome it but won't go out of my way to look for one.

As for fame:

> I don't care in the least for recognition. In fact I loathe any personal publicity.

The serenity of these days was soon to be terminated by violence, and the poetic dream of a spiritual Ireland suffered a severe blow. Introduction of a Home Rule Bill in the House of Commons aroused resentment in Northern Ireland, and the Ulster Volunteers were formed in December 1912. The leader, Sir Edward Carson, defied legality: "Drilling is illegal. . .the Volunteers are illegal. . .and the Government dare not interfere. . . . Don't be afraid of illegalities." His fellow conspirator, Captain James Craig, predicted for 1914 "Home Rule in May, Civil War in June. . .and the smash up of the Empire in August." The last of these proved true, for the British Empire was to meet its great test in August 1914.

3

Decline

Seldom have current history and literature merged so closely as in the Ireland of 1913 to 1923. A.E. discovered a new voice, that of public indignation, with his manifestoes of national conscience. In the summer of 1913, after several months of labor unrest, William Martin Murphy, chairman of the United Tramway Company, promised a raise of a shilling a week, and denounced the leader, James Larkin, as aspiring to become "the labour dictator of Dublin." The Dublin slums at this time were reputedly the worst in Europe; it was later revealed that 21,000 families were living in one-room flats.

The drama of this crisis has been recaptured in a collection of documents, *1913: Jim Larkin and the Dublin Lock-out* (1964). It contains an imposing list of protesters. In addition to Larkin there are four figures of the 1916 Rising (Constance Markievicz, Tom Clarke, James Connolly, and Padraic Pearse), the writers Yeats, A.E., Stephens, and O'Casey, and the painter Sir William Orpen. As an Irish friend said to me, "When the chips were down, all of them were on the right side."

Murphy's dismissal of union members from the tram company led to a strike during Horse Show Week in August. This action, in the words of W. P. Ryan's *The Irish Labour Movement* (1919), aroused "the indignation of snobs and pleasure-hunters, who thought it positively scandalous on the part of the 'lower classes' to interfere with the distractions of the rich." Public demonstrations, police attacks, arrests and deaths followed, but perhaps most cruel of all was the decision by a federation of some four hundred employers to lock out 24,000 workers. Ryan characterizes A.E.'s "memorable letter" as "sure to be the most enduring monument of the struggle." With a directness that recalls Zola's in the Dreyfus case, A.E. addressed "The Masters of Dublin" (Murphy was president of the local chamber of commerce, founder of the *Irish Independent,* and creator of the Employer's Federation, which had forced the lockout). The letter, published in the *Irish Times* (October 7, 1913), charges that "like all aristocracies, you tend to grow blind in long authority." "You do not seem to realize," "You do not seem to read history," "You are bad citizens," "You have allowed the poor to be herded together"—the relentless barrage of accusation continues.

A.E.'s bitterness can be seen in his speech at a mass meeting in London, November 1, attacking the hierarchy for thwarting a plan to remove starving children to England:

> there has sprung up a third party, who are super-human beings, they have so little concern for the body at all, that they assert it is better for children to be starved than to be

moved from the Christian atmosphere of the Dublin slums.
Dublin is the most Christian city in these islands. Its
tottering tenements are holy. The spiritual atmosphere
which pervades them is ample compensation for the
diseases which are there and the food which is not there.

The call to ancient nobility is once more sounded:

> these men are the true heroes of Ireland to-day, they are the
> descendants of Oscar, Cuculain, the heroes of our ancient
> stories. For all their tattered garments, I recognize in these
> obscure men a majesty of spirit.

After six months of widespread misery the strike
collapsed. The chamber of commerce had won, but the
Irish Citizen Army survived, contributing leaders and
members to the 1916 Rising and to the subsequent
struggle for independence. A.E.'s faith in the mind and
spirit of Ireland was shaken. Herbert Howarth, whose
book, *The Irish Writers* (1958), gives the most extended
treatment of A.E.'s controversial prose, quotes a letter
of 1913:

> The land is shaking with the tramp of volunteers. Labour is
> drilling. The Hibernians are drilling, so are the Sinn Feiners.
> The Ulster men are also at it still. Ireland seems to have
> forgotten it had any brains. . . .I am all for other methods;
> but all my friends are so enthusiastic that I can only look
> on and hope that the Lord means something good for this
> unfortunate country.

As the Home Rule Bill was becoming imminent,
Rudyard Kipling, himself of Irish descent, turned the
drumbeat of his verse into a Protestant diatribe against
Irish hopes for political sovereignty. His poem, "Ulster,"
published April 9, 1912, contains these lines:

We know the wars prepared
On every peaceful home,
We know the hells declared
For such as serve not Rome—

The same inflammatory language is heard sixty years later, and had been heard at the instigation of the Orange Lodges in Ulster a quarter-century before. It echoes Lord Randolph Churchill's warning of 1886: "Ulster will fight, Ulster will be right," a slogan which spread throughout the area.

A.E. struck back in a denunciation which brought down upon Kipling the accumulated power of Irish culture:

You have blood of our race in you, and you may, perhaps, have some knowledge of Irish sentiment. You have offended against one of our noblest literary traditions in the way you have published your thoughts.

He taunted Kipling on "making profit out of the perils of your country" and reminded him that "In Ireland every poet we honour has dedicated his genius to his country without gain." Kipling would be unworthy of being answered were it not that "there have been hours when the immortal in you secured your immortality in literature, when you ceased to see life with that hard cinematograph eye of yours, and saw with the eyes of the spirit"—a most apt metaphor. As for presumed Catholic intolerance:

I am a person whose whole being goes into a blaze at the thought of oppression of faith, and yet I think my Catholic countrymen more tolerant than those who hold the faith I was born in. I am a heretic judged by their standards, a heretic who has written and made public his heresies, and I have never suffered in friendship or found my heresies an obstacle in life.

The Irish Volunteers had been organized at a rally on November 25, 1913, an outgrowth of the Gaelic League. In recounting these times a writer finds himself literally overwhelmed with political and military events, such as gun-running north and south, drilling by various groups, the 1916 Rising, executions of the leaders, imprisonment without trial, resistance to conscription, the Convention, Sinn Fein election victories, the first Dail in January 1919, the Anglo-Irish War, the Treaty of December 1921, the Provisional and Free State governments, the Civil War, and the return of the Republican representatives to the Dail in 1927.

Like Yeats, A.E. was startled by the suddenness of the Rising; like Yeats he wrote a poem in the same tenor, "Salutation," privately printed the following January. It opens in a manner surprisingly similar to that of Yeats's magnificent "Easter, 1916," both poems expressing earlier indifference to the Volunteer movement: "Their dream had left me numb and cold," the poet admits, yet he salutes those names, as did Yeats:

> Here's to you, Pearse, your dream not mine
> . . . .
> Here's to you, Connolly, my man. . . .

The conclusion evokes the complex currents which contributed to the Rising:

>   the confluence of dreams
>   That clashed together in our night,

One river born from many streams,
Roll in one blaze of blinding light.

In these troubled times A.E. meditated on his concepts of *The National Being,* published in September 1916. The volume is both a logical presentation of policy and a summons to human aspiration. "Civilizations are externalizations of the soul and character of races"—such is the premise. Partisan strife arises from neglect of ideal concerns:

> Men who love Ireland ignobly brawl about her in their cups, quarrel about her with their neighbor, allow no freedom of thought of her or service of her other than their own, take to the cudgel and the rifle, and join sectarian orders or lodges to ensure that Ireland will be made in their own ignoble image.

There is still hope, however; A.E. regains his almost insuperable optimism. The Lock-out revealed nobility among the laborers, who would not sign away their freedom, but instead "Quietly and grimly. . .took through hunger the path to the Heavenly City."

As A.E. sketches his national policy we see his practical sense beneath the dreaming exterior. In the hope to "carve an Attica out of Ireland," a program must unite urban and rural interests. No one as yet has taken "the trouble to think out a form of government befitting Irish circumstance and character," which the author defines as "intensely democratic in economic theory" with a contrasting "aristocratic freedom of thought."

In our own day, when talk of reordering priorities is on every tongue, A.E.'s vision of public service seems several generations ahead of its time. A civilian army could establish playgrounds, gardens, hospitals; reclaim and reforest wastelands; build "schools, picture-galleries, public halls, libraries, and a thousand enterprises which now hang fire because at present labour for public service is the most expensive labour." Such a corps "would create a real brotherhood in work, just as the army creates in its own way a brotherhood between men in the same regiments."

He challenges the Irish to "direct into the right channel all that national capacity for devotion to causes for which they are famed." Thus would the "heaven-born" goals "of freedom, of brotherhood, of power, of justice, of beauty" create "that inner unity which constitutes the national being."

The time for rational discussion was already passing. Bands of volunteers were drilling, and soon played their roles in the Rising. In the month following the execution of the fifteen leaders, A.E. wrote to Mrs. Hinkson:

> One's heart is very heavy. Everybody seems suffering from a kind of suppressed hysteria but it will go off I suppose. I think Ireland is in a bad way and I see no hope at present.

He continued: "and Lloyd George is no good. . .a sheer muddler." Lloyd George was more than "a sheer muddler," as his actions were soon to show. His summoning an Irish Convention in 1917 was proof of his wiliness in dealing with an inflammable situation. In the first place, to the Prime Minister the separation of Ulster was implicit. Secondly, delegates were appointed, not elected. Arthur Griffith, founder of the independent

Sinn Fein party and a keen controversialist, saw through the scheme at once; in his journal, *Nationality,* he wrote (June 2, 1917) that Lloyd George "summons a Convention, and guarantees that a small minority of people will not be bound by its decision, and thus, having secured its failure, he is armed to assure the world that England left the Irish to settle the question of government for themselves and that they could not agree." Sinn Fein was offered only five of the 101 nominations, though it was the strongest party in Ireland. It ignored the invitation; labor boycotted it, as did the All for Ireland League. The result was, in Dorothy MacArdle's words, that "Ninety per cent of the Convention were men who had already consented to Partition."

Herbert Howarth comments on A.E.'s polemical style: "AE could not always write with. . .force, but he struck it sufficiently often to command attention throughout his middle life." In his letters of May 26 to May 28, 1917, printed in the *Irish Times* and later as a booklet, *Thoughts for a Convention,* he displays other qualities—reasonableness and clarity. These features are rather surprising in a mystic, but again the author reveals his many-sided nature. Had the voice of A.E. prevailed, a Civil War in Ireland and a half century of bitter feeling and violence might have been avoided.

He begins:

> There are moments in history when by the urgency of circumstances every one in a country is drawn from normal pursuits to consider the affairs of the nation.

His basic divergence from the much-disputed Treaty of 1921 is in rejecting the separation of the northern counties: "If any partition of Ireland is contemplated, this will intensify the bitterness now existing." He proposes a provincial government like that of Canada, with guarantees of civil and religious liberty, complete autonomy in local government, competitive examinations for civil service, and no compulsory Gaelic. Some such solution might satisfy both extremes:

> both would obtain substantially what they desire, the Ulster Unionists, that safety for their interests and provision for Ireland's unity with the commonwealth of dominions inside the empire; the Nationalists, that power they desire to create an Irish civilization. . . .

The result "would not be imperialism in the ancient sense but a federal union of independent nations to protect national liberties." He closes with an appeal to the higher motives of man:

> We in Ireland like the rest of the world must rise above ourselves and our differences if we are to manifest the genius which is in us, and play a noble part in world history.

Unfortunately, such reasonableness was not to be manifested. The Convention dragged to a weary and indecisive close in April 1918, after fifty-one sessions. A.E. had resigned two months before, "because I could do no more there," as he wrote to St. John Ervine, in a letter quoted by John Eglinton. His explanation to Sir Horace Plunkett was more explicit. In refusing to sit, "The Sinn Feiners were right in their intuitions from the start." He expressed regret that he had ever consented to becoming involved:

> If I had followed my intuition from the first I would have

remained away also. A man must be either an Irishman or an Englishman in this matter. I am Irish.

The date of this letter, February 3, 1918, marked the end of A.E.'s political influence, or rather the beginning of the end. English manpower was being drained on the Western Front, and conscription had been introduced, though not yet in Ireland. Lloyd George was in a desperate position, forced by circumstances to ignore the steadily rising Sinn Fein power in Ireland. The timing could hardly have been worse for England. Just one day after receipt of the Irish Convention report the House of Commons reconvened, and Lloyd George announced a Man-Power Bill which authorized conscription in Ireland at any time by an Order in Council. The entire Irish Party voted against the bill, which passed on April 16. Within two days a "National Cabinet" met in Dublin, with representatives from the Parliamentary Party (who had left Westminster), from Sinn Fein, and from other groups. Eamon de Valera proposed a resolution which passed unanimously:

> Taking our stand on Ireland's separate and distinct nationhood and affirming the principle of liberty. . .we deny the right of the British Government. . .to impose compulsory military service in Ireland against the clearly expressed will of the Irish people. . . .
> It is in direct violation of the rights of small nationalities to self-determination, which even the Prime Minister of England—now preparing to employ naked militarism and force his Act upon Ireland—himself officially announced as an essential condition for peace at the Peace Congress.

A.E. wrote a long letter, published in the *Manchester Guardian,* May 10, 1918, in which he attempted to explain the Irish position and to mollify English antagonism. "I write as an Irishman interpreting my own people, but not, I hope, without understanding and sympathy for the people of England. . .for I know there is hardly a household in Great Britain to which death has not drawn nigh, and its people are bitter at heart about my people." His eloquent defense of the Irish, with its warning of "a hate which will be inextinguishable, lasting from generation to generation," is a noble statement. It was published as a pamphlet, *Conscription for Ireland* (May 1918), and is reprinted in Denson's edition of A.E.'s *Letters,* together with other of Russell's Open Letters on public matters.

Despite the mounting ferocity of the Anglo-Irish War (January 1919-July 1921), and the even more violent Civil War (June 1922-May 1923), A.E. published a half dozen pamphlets on political and economic issues, but his power was waning.

A year after the Treaty, the Provisional Government was followed by that of the Irish Free State. Arthur Griffith, head of the Provisional Government, had died in August 1922 of heart failure only ten days before the murder of his successor, Michael Collins, and the leadership went to William Cosgrave, Minister of Local Government. Oliver Gogarty, close friend of the late Griffith, proposed A.E. and Yeats as members of the Free State Senate. A.E. declined. It meant removal from politics, but it undoubtedly saved him from subjection to the campaign of arson, assassination, and kidnapping carried on by the Irregulars. Donal O'Sullivan's definitive *The Irish Free State and Its Senate* (1940) lists twenty-one such raids carried out between December 6, 1922, and March 26, 1923.

A.E. had withdrawn from politics, but his *The National Being,* twice reprinted in 1918, had made of him a creator of the conscience of the race. Ernest Boyd writes of this book in his 1922 revision of *Ireland's Literary Renaissance* (1916):

> It was read alike by British statesmen, Sinn Fein leaders, and the general public; it established the author's fame as one of the few clear and absolutely disinterested minds engaged upon the Irish problem, as part of the general problem of humanity's evolution towards a new social order.

A.E. was to discuss the larger problem of man's social evolution in two fictional symposia, *The Interpreters* (1922) and *The Avatars* (1933). The Irish setting is now only the foreground to a wider political question. The first book adumbrates a faint hope that diversities of belief may somehow become reconciled. It is dedicated to Stephen MacKenna, "FOR THE DELIGHT I HAVE IN HIS NOBLE TRANSLATION OF PLOTINUS." Plotinus is invoked by one of the characters as spokesman for "a harmony of identities":

> I think it was old Plotinus who said that when each utters his own voice all are brought into accord by universal law.

The aerial bombardment which takes place while the men huddle in their prison anticipates a scene from the Battle of Britain. Among the participants are a socialist Culain, the historian Brehon, modeled upon O'Grady (whose history "had unveiled so extraordinary a past. . .that his work became an object of passionate study by his countrymen"), an industrialist, Heyt, and a

cynical aesthete, Leroy, undoubtedly based on George
Moore. Leroy poses a central question, only to mock it.
"What relation have the politics of time to the politics
of eternity?" he asks, a statement used by A.E. as one
of the book's epigraphs. The question is tossed aside in
keeping with Leroy's disbelief in divine intervention: "I
do not think the ridge-pole of the universe is so fragile
as to be shaken by our rubbing ourselves against it." His
is an epicurean stance, "the intensive cultivation of
human life" with no cosmic purpose.

A.E.'s point of view is divided between two of the
prisoners, the idealist Lavelle and the artist Rian. Lavelle
traces his development from mythological vision
through national history to poetic tradition:

> These divine visitations have been the dominant influence
> in our literature so that our poets have sung of their
> country as the shadow of Heaven. The hills were sacred, the
> woods were sacred. . .because of that eternal beauty which
> was seen behind them. . . .Political thought with us too has
> been more inspired by the national culture than by the
> economic needs which almost completely inspire political
> activity elsewhere.

Rian sees in Greek and Egyptian temples an indication
of national being: "The people who saw such beauty
and magnificence must have been proud and uplifted in
heart." His aspiration is creativity:

> I desired passionately to build the palaces and cities of
> dream here on the earth, and I wanted the prophets of
> beauty like Lavelle to prepare the way in people's souls.

The dilemma is the role of force in history: "How can
right find its appropriate might?" asks Lavelle (another

of the epigraphs). It seems that A.E. is finding,
reluctantly, the hold that force has upon man's imagination. As the symposium ends, the artist Rian expresses
his own doubts:

> I wonder if I had heard all this a year ago would it have
> made any difference. It can make little difference now.

The Avatars (1933) shows a further loss of con-
fidence, a sense that the traditional vision of Ireland was
indeed a thing of the past. The author's preface conveys
his discouragement: "I have, I fear, delayed too long the
writing of this, for as I grow old the moon of fantasy
begins to set confusedly with me." The book "has not
the spiritual gaiety I desired for it." It could have been
different, years ago:

> The friends with whom I once spoke of such things are
> dead or gone far from me. If they were with me, out of
> dream, vision and intuition shared between us, I might have
> made the narrative to glow. As it is, I have only been able
> to light my way with my own flickering lantern.

The eternal cry of age is here, awareness of failing
energy and of the loss of former companions.

Subtitled "A Futurist Fantasy," the book is a
fictional parallel to A.E.'s visionary landscapes. The
artist, Paul, fleeing from the inhuman grime of the city,
meets in the western hills his friend Conaire, a rhapsodic
thinker. Passing references to characters and ideas in
The Interpreters indicate that this fable is intended as a
sequel; Conaire welcomes his visitor, of whose coming
he had had premonitions, and echoes Lavelle's awareness of the intermingling of human and divine:

"There is a prologue in heaven to that. . . .I know why you and I are what we are. I know why Lavelle fashioned poetry out of legend and coloured it with fairy. I know why Brehon turned to a language which had become almost a tradition, and why the enthusiasts of a rural civilisation began their labours. They were all forerunners."

As Paul sits at his easel, a supernaturally beautiful boy appears. The child has a spiritual influence on people: "They have no light in their minds unless I blow into them. . . .I imagine them dancing in curves like the clouds and they begin to dance." This fairy child, Aodh, runs lightly over the hill, "the golden curls in a last flashing against the blue sky." Visions, dreams, and legends hurry by, all pointing toward a new awakening in which man once more can rise to imagination and beauty.

As this pastoral symposium continues, we are introduced to a poet who may derive in part from Yeats. Gregor is described as having "a kind of lofty, dark, exasperated nobility" rooted in self-conflict. This struggle against oneself suggests Yeats's concepts of Mask and Anti-Self:

"Though he is at war with the civilisation where he was once a great figure, his enemies truly are not without but within the house of the soul. Because of that intimate conflict he is becoming a much greater writer."

Unwittingly, A.E. has here come close to expressing his own basic shortcomings, whether in painting or poetry. Yeats had lamented A.E.'s innocence of Evil, and this lack of contrast leads to monotony and repetitiousness.

As it is, we must take the word of Conaire that the appearance of the supernatural beings is already becoming legendary. One might retort that such divine avatars must be believed to be seen, but the world usually reverses the notion.

For six and a half years, A.E. edited the weekly *Irish Statesman,* often writing a great deal of the copy himself under several different initials. This journal, and the *Dublin Magazine,* edited by his old friend, Seumus O'Sullivan (James Sullivan Starkey), presented the best of Irish culture during the twenties. The diversity of A.E.'s journal is astonishing. John Eglinton writes:

> In a single number we find (all written by himself) well-informed notes on current topics, home and foreign; at least one brilliant leading article; a literary or philosophical "causerie"; a poem; book-reviews; besides that part of the paper which continued the work of the *Irish Homestead.*

Monk Gibbon put it in one sentence: "His passionate interest in ideas gave him zeal for almost any topic." Gibbon's collection of essays and aphorisms from the *Irish Statesman,* in which the sentence above is to be found, appeared in 1938 as *The Living Torch.* The sections of this book show the editor's versatility: Literature and Criticism, Men and Women, Politics of Time and Eternity, More Criticism, Aphorism, Civics and Rural Economy. Journalism by its very nature tends to be ephemeral, but, as Gibbon says, "In the torrent which poured from his pen there were continually being thrown out these precious stones, crystal clear, proof against time, as well as the rainbow effects of airy fancy, formed as it were by the spray as it fell."

Though presumably nonpartisan, the *Statesman's* aim was to support the Free State government. Plunkett had founded the Dominion League (1919-1920) which advocated dominion status, and in 1925 he expressed delight in A.E.'s editorial efforts and "in the guidance he has given to the Government of the Free State and in the way he has protected them from the Republicans." Whatever the political tone, there can be no doubt as to A.E.'s energy. More than 650 signed pieces by him are listed in Edward Doyle Smith's massive index (Doctoral Dissertation, University of Washington, Seattle, 1966). Unsigned articles and notes would certainly double this total. Of the 425 poems printed, 65 are by A.E., 25 by Gogarty, 23 by Frank O'Connor, and 18 by F. R. Higgins.

The final number, April 12, 1930, contained farewell notes by A.E. and Sir Horace Plunkett. A.E. acknowledged that the closing of the *Statesman* completed a major work of his life and brought to an end an important cultural movement "which began at the latter end of the last century and which by now [has] almost spent its force." He recorded his fondest wish, to be remembered as "the friend of the Irish poets, those who make the soul of a nation."

Disillusionment with the new, lower middle-class Ireland, the death of friends, and his sense of declining powers made deep shadows during his last ten years. His editorial associate, friend, and neighbor, the witty and charming Susan L. Mitchell, died in 1926, his wife in 1932 ("She could endure suffering," he wrote, "better than any I have known"), and, in the next month, his patron Sir Horace Plunkett. A harrowing experience was his arrival in Donegal to spend a holiday with his friends, the Kingsley Porters, to find that Porter had drowned accidentally that very morning. Mrs. Porter recalled his sympathy as he read to her in the evenings, occasionally peering up "tenderly as a mother, hoping I had fallen asleep."

In July of 1933 he sold his Rathgar home, the center of his world and haven for two generations of writers. With characteristic generosity he invited friends to share his treasured possessions. Frank O'Connor recalled, in *My Father's Son* (1968):

> for him to give up everything—his house, his books, his pictures, his friends—was already a sort of death.

A.E. had asked him to "take whatever I wanted," and when O'Connor did not come, F. R. Higgins was sent to bring him along:

> Russell's face was like a tragic mask as he showed other friends about the rooms and let them take his little treasures. . . .I told Russell that I did not want to take anything of his, and he said in a broken voice, "You mustn't leave without taking something. I put aside a set of the Jack Yeats' broadsheets for you. I know you admire Jack Yeats. Do please take them."

One final honor was to be his. President Roosevelt's New Deal sought out the old wisdom, and A.E. was invited to the United States by Henry A. Wallace, Secretary of Agriculture (later Vice-President, and Progressive Party nominee in 1948). On his arrival in December 1934 no one seems to have sensed that he would live only seven months more. Alan Denson prints a letter by Judge Richard Campbell of January 17, 1935, in which the writer says "I soon found, in other words, that his mind had lost none of its sweep and that he was as mentally and physically alive and vigorous as ever." Within six weeks he was en route to England, a dying man. In July an operation revealed that his condition was incurable. One of his last letters, written two days before his death, was to Henry Wallace; the Secretary hoped for his return in the fall: "we need that touch of beauty and interpretation of reality which he alone can give." A.E. wrote his farewell to Wallace on July 15, 1935:

This is to say goodbye to you. . . .To you dear Henry, as to myself, death does not make much matter. We understand each other. I hope for you a great career in your country. Give my kind regards to your wife. Collier and Wilson will understand I was not trying to escape from any work I could do. It was really that I felt incapable. Yours ever, AE.

4

A.E. as a Theosophist

A.E. seems to have been a natural visionary. When he was sixteen or seventeen he was struck by visions of preternatural lights and figures. Of these experiences, he wrote:

> But the luminous quality gradually became normal in me, and at times in meditation there broke in on me an almost intolerable lustre of light, pure and shining faces, dazzling processions of figures, most ancient, ancient places and peoples, and landscapes lovely as the lost Eden. (*The Candle of Vision*, p. 28)

These visions were so compelling that A.E. studied to increase his skill in meditation; he sought solitude but was delighted with friends like W. B. Yeats. Out of his visions A.E. later constructed his poems, paintings, philosophy, and his ambition to work for the spiritual rejuvenation of Ireland. While many Dubliners scoffed at his claim to have seen Celtic gods, heroes, and fairies, A.E. seems never to have doubted the reality of his inner illuminations.

One of A.E.'s friends, Charles Johnston, recalled the

atmosphere of the late 1880s, a time when several
Theosophists "began to seek the small old paths the
seers know. . . . That young enthusiasm and hourly joy
of living was one of old destiny's gracious presents, a
brightness to be remembered. . ." (*From the
Upanishads*, pp. vii, viii). This brightness remembered
permeated A.E.'s verse and prose throughout his life.
For instance, in commenting on an anthology of Irish
verse edited by Rolleston and Brooke in 1900, A.E.
thought the book ". . .should help us in what I think is
the destiny of the Irish writers—to spiritualise English
literature" (D., Ms. 8). Also, in November 1913, A.E.
wrote to Stephen MacKenna that he was troubled by
the drilling of Edward Carson's Ulster Volunteers, the
plight of the Dublin laborers in the Lock-out, and the
threats of the Sinn Feiners. A.E. recalled a vision of
twenty years earlier, one of a series on the future of
Ireland:

> I saw a figure descending from heaven and standing on the
> earth, and at that moment a mother held a child in her lap.
> Then I saw the old queen, Victoria, toppling from her
> throne, and other things—then a gigantic figure stalked
> across Ireland beating a drum and there were fights and
> alarms and smoke and burnings; then after a silence the
> mountains flung up their rays as Brigid saw in her
> visions. . . . I wonder will I see the avatar when he begins his
> labour of freeing Ireland. (D., Ms. 227)

In April 1896, A.E. had had a vision of an avatar living
in a whitewashed cottage in the west of Ireland who had
come to restore spirituality in Ireland. But in 1913 he
was saddened because military and political violence
would destroy any chance of the revolution he desired.

A.E. discovered for himself that Ireland was a sacred

land. Like other Theosophists he entertained an ambition to go to India, but once he became acquainted with Celtic myths and adapted these myths to the Theosophical world-view, he gave his spiritual aspirations an Irish setting. He readily interpreted events like the Easter Rising of 1916 as an impulse of the oversoul: ". . .acting through many men and speaking through many voices, and to make it a record of national culture; that is all the deeds and visions and imaginations of Irishmen where they have acted beyond themselves or seen beyond themselves, where in deed or thought one surmises a deeper being" (D., Ms. 296). Like Yeats, A.E. searched for dominant images that governed individuals and nations. He believed in a subtle commerce between the world spirit, the *anima mundi*, and the individual. In 1932, for instance, he thought the western seaboard from Donegal to Kerry was favored by the gods: "I think there is some emanation flowing out of the earth spirit there, . . .emanations like those the sybils breathed and uttered oracles out of the inspiration. The country about Ben Bulben in Sligo is I think charged with some mysterious life" (D., Ms. 549).

A.E.'s hopes for the spiritual renewal of Ireland reached a peak in 1897 when he wrote two pamphlets— "The Future of Ireland and the Awakening of the Fires" and "Ideals in Ireland: Priest or Hero?" These pamphlets were not reprinted because he felt they would be inappropriate to his work as an organizer of cooperative creameries and banks; he told Yeats that they were pieces of blazing paganism which would not increase his usefulness in Ireland (D., Ms. 370).

In "Ideals in Ireland: Priest or Hero?" A.E. calls the chief failure of the Irish their submissiveness to the

Church. The tyranny of the Church poisons Irish life, especially in political affairs in which leaders bow to the Church, as they did in the Parnell affair. A.E. holds out a remedy: the Irish should emulate heroes like Cuchulain and Oisin, their true ancestors. A.E. asked the Irish to consider their own land, not Palestine, as their sacred country. Christianity became corrupt, he said, as soon as it was placed in the hands of the priests, who exploited a fear of hell-fire. But the Irish are heirs to a tradition older than Christianity, one which is still available in the Celtic myths. Unfortunately the heroic mood has faded from memory, but Irish countrymen still see enchanted lights in mountains and valleys, and they hear fairy bells from the underland to which the Danaans withdrew. Now the Irish must see and hear for themselves and cast off the authority of the priest, an enemy of the imagination:

> Now the country is alive with genius, flashing out everywhere, in conversation even of the lowest; but we cannot point to imaginative work of any importance produced in Ireland which has owed its inspiration to the priestly teaching. The genius of the Gael could not find itself in their doctrine; though above all things mystical it could not pierce its way into the departments of super-nature where their theology pigeon-holes the souls of the damned and the blessed.

After centuries of slavery, the genius of the Gael has aroused itself; the Irish will drive out priests and regain heroic consciousness.

Since A.E.'s death in 1935, a few writers like Monk Gibbon, Alan Denson, and recently Henry Summerfield and William Daniels, have separated fact from Dublin reminiscence to present an accurate view of A.E.'s life and beliefs. One promising approach lies in Monk Gibbon's view that A.E. lacked the requisite humility of the mystic who tries to immerse himself in the Deity. According to Gibbon, A.E. endeavored to find himself, believing that if he found himself he would thereby find the divine principle. Thus A.E. shares the quest of those artists and poets exploring the self and its resources, seeking, in Jung's phrase, an integration of personality. While Yeats makes a descent into personality. A.E. concentrates on the transcendent and ethereal. A.E.'s search for self is evident in his methods of meditation, his belief that poetry requires a transfiguration of self, and his concern for cultural images that aid or obstruct the development of the self. A.E.'s studies in Theosophy may be regarded in large measure as a pursuit of the latent powers of the self.

A.E. gradually shifted from a private visionary to an active member of the Dublin Lodge of the Theosophical Society. In letters to Carrie Rea, his young confidante in Armagh, A.E. described the growth of his beliefs. In October 1887, he called himself a Theosophist because he believed in "internal illumination" and he found that his intuitions about many things agree with the teachings of the Theosophists (D., Ms. 8). But in February of the same year he acknowledged only a slight acquaintance with Theosophical literature: "I have read no Theosophical books except a little book of about ten or twelve pages called 'Light on the Path' and 'Idyll of the Lotus,' which I am glad you are going to read." In the same letter he listed the Theosophical teachings he approved: "...first,—that the spirit in us is God—

secondly—that we will finally be absorbed in him—
thirdly, that the animals and plants will have their
chance of Nirvana when we are out of the road" (D.,
Ms. 5). After death, A.E. continues, one does not lose
individuality but consciousness of himself as distinct
from others. If man believes in one essence of nature,
and that of God, he can accept the idea that this essence
was created before he was born or that it existed in
idleness since eternity. He must then agree that he
existed before physical birth, that character is the result
of thoughts and actions of previous incarnations. For
A.E. reincarnation accounted for the suffering of
mankind, such as that of children in slums.

As a Dubliner A.E. received instruction in Theosophy
from several sources besides Madame Blavatsky's *Isis
Unveiled* (1877) and *The Secret Doctrine* (1888), books
which he praised to the end of his life. In several works
A. P. Sinnett explains the doctrines of Theosophy: *The
Occult World* (1881), *Esoteric Buddhism* (1883), and
The Growth of the Soul (1896). A discussion of
Esoteric Buddhism at Professor Edward Dowden's home
stimulated several Dubliners, including W. B. Yeats, to
found a Hermetic Society in 1885. The Dublin Lodge of
the Theosophical Society received its charter in 1886.
For the general reader, Sinnett's books provide a lucid
approach to Theosophy, but they lack the clutter of
myth, arcane knowledge, and diatribes against scientists
and Christians that enliven the Blavatsky books.
Another Theosophical mentor was Mohini Chatterji,
remembered in a poem by W. B. Yeats. George Moore
wrote: "A.E. had gone to him [Mohini] instinctively as
to a destiny and a few months later the Upanishads and

the Vedas were born again in verse and prose. . ." (*Hail and Farewell*, 2: 22-30) But Moore characteristically overdramatizes Chatterji's role, for he was but one of many influences on A.E. at this time.

A.E. joined the Dublin Lodge in 1888 and the Esoteric Section on December 8, 1890. This latter group was created not only for intensive study and meditation but also to provide disciples directly under control of Madame Blavatsky. Within these Theosophical circles, A.E. found methods for meditating and for developing his visionary powers, and obtained the friendship of several young men and women dissatisfied with the commercial spirit, imperial politics, and official Christianity. Despite his long hours at Pim's store, A.E. worked zealously for Theosophical causes. He lectured on topics such as "The Higher Mind" and "First Steps in Occultism." He published poems and stories in Theosophical journals, and collaborated with James Pryse on a series, "The Enchantment of Cuchillin," with illustrations by A.E. When *The Irish Theosophist* combined with *The Grail* in 1897, A.E. served as an editor. He made his home in the Household, a layman's monastery, where he lived from 1891 to 1897. During this period he developed rapidly as a writer, speaker, and organizer, changing from a rather awkward, sometimes incoherent youth to a man who had acquired the Emersonian virtue of self-reliance.

The Household must have seemed a strange group in the Dublin of the 1890s. The *chelas* or disciples lived at 3 Upper Ely Place, just off Merrion Square and St. Stephen's Green. Apparently the Household organized itself, but the owners and masters of the house were

Frederick and Annie Dick. Dick, an engineer, had a practical, intellectual approach to life, and his wife served as the bright spirit of the group. A.E. and others praised her graciousness and self-sacrifice. The men followed strictures developed by Madame Blavatsky: celibacy, no liquor, no smoking, and no meat. They devoted themselves to reading the sacred books, especially those of the Orient, to practicing meditation, to holding meetings for members of the Lodge, and editing *The Irish Theosophist*. Generally there were only six or seven residents of the Household at a time. These included A.E., Malcolm Magee, the brother of John Eglinton; James Pryse, Charles Johnston, Charles Weekes, and Violet North, whom A.E. married in 1898.

A.E. withdrew from the Theosophical Society in March 1898, but he associated himself with a Hermetic Society for many years. A.E.'s Hermetic Society met at first in his home, but later moved to a room in Dawson Street. On October 20, 1904, a charter was granted for a Second Dublin Lodge, which continued until 1909. From 1909 until 1933 A.E. continued as the leader of the Hermetic Society. The meetings generally opened with passages from *The Secret Doctrine* but then moved to discussions of Celtic myth, literature, and one of A.E.'s major topics, the national being of Ireland. Through A.E.'s Society writers like James Stephens, whom A.E. called the best of companions in the dedication to *The Candle of Vision*, were introduced to Eastern writings.

A.E.'s understanding of Theosophy was inescapably influenced by that of its founder, Madame Blavatsky. In her account Theosophy is based on a synthesis of Oriental, pre-socratic, neoplatonic, and medieval mysticism. It incorporates all myths and symbolisms and considers each an expression of the original divine revelation. Madame Blavatsky counters Christianity with the exotic, comprehensive beliefs of the Orient; in response to Darwin, Tyndall, and Huxley she proposed an evolution of the spirit. Insisting on personal revelation as opposed to intellectual acceptance of doctrine, she argued that the material order has only a relative reality; ultimate reality rests entirely in the Absolute. Each soul lives in exile from the Absolute and is in the process of returning to its homeland by passing through numerous incarnations, each a stage of purification.

A.E.'s adaptation of Theosophy appears in *The Candle of Vision* (1918). A curious work, the book is in part a spiritual autobiography and an apologia for a mystic who follows his own synthesis of tradition rather than the teachings of a church or school. In discussing his visions, A.E. hardly refers to other religious writers and ignores Theosophical sources. Some chapters have promising headings such as "Intuition," "Language of the Gods," and "Have Imaginations Body?" but they often trail off in vague comments and unanalyzed personal experience. But a note of simple integrity runs through the book; he leaves the impression, often in florid prose, of a man with unshakable faith in his own visions, of a man earnestly striving to make clear his extraordinary inner illuminations.

The Candle of Vision contains a brief chapter on Celtic Cosmogenesis, thereby fulfilling an old ambition. In 1903 A.E. sent Yeats this proposal:

> I am going to do the cosmogony first, and then go to the local mysteries and the beings seen as the Tuatha. I will also deal with mountains, islands, fountains, and symbols. . . I

am sure I will irritate a great many people by then as I
intend to show incidentally how much more poetic and
complete the system is than our orthodox faith. Any
scholar who reads it will go quite mad. (*Letters of A.E. to
W.B. Yeats*, p. 38)

A.E. tried to "reconstruct the Celtic vision of Heaven
and Earth as I believe it was known to the Druids and
bardic seers." In A.E.'s version, all creation stems from
the boundless Lir, who contains the spiritual form of
spirit, energy, and matter. All the gods are cradled in
Lir, celebrating an endless Feast of Age. Lir's son
Mananan MacLir, the second logos, the source of
conscious life, serves as the spirit of the universe, the
divine imagination. Although Lir is the root of life, the
forms proceed from Mananan, whose bounty is
expressed in the sacred hazel, the Celtic tree of life.
Divinities and indeed all forms of life branch out from
the sacred tree in series of seven. The third logos, Dana,
is the mother of the gods, the first spiritual form of
matter and hence Beauty. She is the patroness of A.E.'s
thought and work. Men fail to recognize Dana on earth
because a veil, the Akasa of Theosophy or the ether of
the Greeks, screens her from mortal sight. A.E. pene-
trated this veil, seeing Dana as "that divine compassion
which exists beyond and is the final arbiter of the
justice of the gods. Her heart will be in ours when ours
forgive" (p. 161).

A.E. sometimes writes in terms of a fourfold universe: (1) the god-world, the home of Lir, a region
beyond the vision of the seers; (2) the heaven-world, the
Land of the Ever Living, the Land of the Youth of the
Celtic twilight; (3) the mid-world, the Gaelic World of
the Waters, the home of the shining beings, of ele-

mentals, nymphs, and dryads; and (4) the earth-world with Dana as its deity. At present, gods dwell in the earth-world ignorant of their past, living in peasants, fishermen, and others.

Even in the earth-world, the divine signature is evident in nature. Spiritual paths connecting the four realms are partially clarified in A.E.'s comments on Angus, the god of love. In the god-world, Angus plays a tympan and has birds, souls, circling his head. In the process of creation, when the fountain beneath the hazel is broken, when the One becomes Many, Angus appears as a primary creative force: "An energy of love or eternal desire has gone forth which seeks through a myriad forms of illusion for the infinite being it has left" (p. 157). Angus, eternal joy, becomes love but is changed to desire and then to earthly passion. In the earth-world he forgets his own divinity as love becomes corrupt and induces spiritual death. Through his several transformations Angus reveals the necessity for purification if one is to reascend the path to the Absolute. In a rare passage on the expense of mysticism, A.E. describes the sacrifice of will and desire the visionary must make:

> To cross that red mid-region between heaven and earth is to undertake labours greater and more painful than those fabled of Hercules. In that red mid-region the martyrdom of the passionate soul, its crucifixion in the spirit, takes place, until all that is gross is etherealized and it yields itself finally in absolute resignation to the ancestral being. It is not easy to stay the will against the desire of the world or to draw ourselves from the attraction of that magnet. *(The Interpreters,* p. 149)

Some Theosophical principles appear frequently in A.E.'s writing: the spiritual nature of matter, the law of maya, and the law of flux. To him all matter was sacred as were all men, but he was not tempted apparently to include in his verse the grotesque, the vulgar, and the repulsive. In his pursuit of the ethereal, he avoided the particularities of nature that fascinated poets like Whitman, Dickinson, and Hopkins. As a youth at Kilmasheogue in the Dublin hills, A.E. first learned of the sacredness of earth, which was revealed to him as a living being:

> and rock and clay were made transparent so that I saw lovelier and lordlier beings than I had known before and was made partner in memory of mighty things, happenings in ages long sunken behind time. (*Song and Its Fountains*, p. 7)

His most sustained tribute to earth appears in the final chapter of *The Candle of Vision,* a prose hymn to its creative forces.

Although A.E. praised the dust beneath his feet, he unfailingly stressed the illusory nature of the physical world under the law of maya. He tried to see through and beyond the material order, discovering a god and hero in a peasant or a Dubliner in Patrick Street. The sight of a young girl evokes thought of the painful incarnations required to produce such fresh beauty. A.E. saw before and after, but seldom did he concentrate on the here and now, his imagination disengaging itself frequently where there was a need for precision. He affirms that men are "but shadow kings that play/ With mirrored majesties and powers" ("Reflections"). Often he sails with hardly a sigh beyond the harsh realities that plague most men. Perhaps A.E.'s composure and his facility for compromise derive from his belief in maya; from the perspective of spirit and eternity human crises often seemed manageable or bearable.

A.E. refers at times to the law of flux, of the duality of creation, but he does not exploit it as an instrument to achieve poetic intensity as Yeats does. In fact, A.E. seldom employs the dialectical process; he avoids extended treatment of evil and hatred, believing, almost too strongly, that we become what we think and hence should avoid explorations of evil. Yet he was not blind to pain and suffering. Although personally a man of great compassion, he accounted philosophically for pain and evil through the laws of karma and reincarnation.

Another principle woven into the fabric of his thought is sacrifice. The highest sacrifice he attributes to spirits who withdraw from the god-world to assist the spiritual evolution of others; these spirits follow the example of Buddha who left Nirvana for spirits imprisoned on earth. A disciplined visionary, A.E. said, might create no karma whatsoever if he acts without hope of reward. As one reaches this pinnacle of spiritual generosity, one's material life may be interpreted as a sacrifice to the Absolute. A.E. was particularly concerned with purifying his motives, even to the point of discontinuing poetry and painting if he could advance his spiritual life by this sacrifice.

As noted previously, he seldom mentioned Theosophy in his later writing. The internecine sniping and the fragmentation of authority within the Society distressed him. By 1909, at the closing of the Second Lodge in Dublin, A.E. gave up hope:

I have begun to despair of any genuine love for art, poetry

or any kind of spiritual imagination in the T.S. [Theosophi-
cal Society] . While it is in a mental state which I can only
describe as the Devachan of a secularist lecturer wherein all
things heavenly are judged by reason and morality and the
flagging horses of emotion are whipped up to duty after
every moral pronouncement. Oh it is dreadful after old
H.P.B. (D., Ms. 169)

In later years, A.E. wanted to be considered a con-
templative and visionary rather than a scholar and
writer. He prized above all his revelations from the inner
light, a knowledge that involved all the powers of man.
As he said in *The Candle of Vision:*

Our religions make promises to be fulfilled beyond the grave
because they have no knowledge now to be put to the test,
but the ancients spake of a divine vision to be attained while
we are yet in the body. (p. 20)

A.E. insisted on the primacy of personal revelation, of
knowledge flowing from the self. He quotes approvingly
a passage from the Enneads of Plotinus: "All the
essences see each other; and interpenetrate each other in
the intimate depth of their nature." And he added a
further description of this knowledge from Spin-
oza: ". . .intuitive knowledge does not consist in being
convinced by reasons but in an immediate union with
the thing itself." (D., Ms. 630) The bond between the
poet or mystic and some aspect of person, place, event,
or the Absolute is described precisely in the phrase,
"immediate union with the thing itself." While A.E.'s
mysticism raises many questions, he did develop his
intuitive powers to a level that is of first importance to
those concerned with the possibilities of consciousness.
Without the program of the Theosophists he would have

had no means of recognizing and developing his inner powers.

5

A. E.'s Poetry

As young men, A.E. and W. B. Yeats were fellow poets, painters, and Theosophists. While Yeats dedicated himself to poetry and building an Irish literary movement, A.E. was reluctant to publish his poems, feeling that his visions would be compromised if the poems were exposed to the public. Yet he had no doubt about the purpose and themes of his poems. For him poetry was to deal only with religious and visionary experience. In 1932 he wrote: ". . .I have tried to make a record of moods which became transparencies into soul or spirit and I have written no poetry without this idea." (D., Ms. 565) Given this position, A.E. compels a reader to forego the ordinary expectation that poetry deal with human passion and nature. He seems to have accepted literally the neo-Platonic teaching that birth is a decline and that the poet must strive to recapture man's original wisdom and happiness.

A.E. made six principal collections of his poems. Three of these belong to his early years when he was active in the Theosophical Society; one was completed when he was editor of *The Irish Statesman*; and two other volumes were published after his retirement as editor in 1930. These dates reflect the intensity of his early visions and the resolution of the older man to put in final form truths acquired in his youth. *Collected Poems* appeared in 1913 and in enlarged forms in 1919 and 1935. His most available work is *Selected Poems* (1935), arranged by the original volumes in which the poems appeared. This gathering, he said, contained the work by which he would like to be remembered. *Collected Poems*, however, has the poems of his first three volumes ordered according to themes, a method which makes it exceptionally difficult to study A.E.'s development as a poet. Although his poems seldom attain the radiance of a unified work of art, they provide an important means for examining the intense experiences of a man dedicated to his visions. In a sense, his poems comprise a spiritual autobiography, the distillation of his inner life.

Since A.E.'s poems have long been out of print, an explication of three poems may illustrate his approach to poetry. A.E. called "The Great Breath," published in his first volume, the most complete statement of his beliefs. Here tone, rhythm, and diction are representative of his early poems:

> Its edges foamed with amethyst and rose,
> Withers once more the old blue flower of day:
> There where the ether like a diamond glows
> Its petals fade away.
>
> A shadowy tumult stirs the dusky air;
> Sparkle the delicate dews, the distant snows;
> The great deep thrills for through it everywhere
> The breath of Beauty blows.

I saw how all the trembling ages past,
Moulded to her by deep and deeper breath,
Neared to the hour when Beauty breathes her last
    And knows herself in death.

This poem, A.E. said, arose from his reading a critique
of Hegel's view that the Absolute becomes self-conscious as it moves through the universe. The critic
argued that no change could occur in a perfect being,
but change might be attributed to the divine mind as it
passed through nature. Later A.E. read an Indian mystic
who related divine mind to primordial substance. A.E.
himself came to regard primordial substance as the
mirror of the divine mind and therefore the Ancient
Beauty. But the poem surprised him; he was uncon-
scious of its creation, and he began to murmur it line by
line. In this instance he felt that philosophical thought
followed the psyche into a spiritual state where genius
makes beauty, joy, dance, and song, and where drab
logic is changed into "colour and music and a rapture of
prophecy" *(Song and Its Fountains,* pp. 69-72).

The "opalhush" language, however, suggests a late
Victorian effort to rise above a daily world plagued with
change, decay, and death. The poet seeks a beauty
beyond nature and hopes to tap a hidden source of
being in metaphors like "The great deep thrills." Yet
A.E.'s statement of intention in this poem may perplex
the reader. He told Charles Weekes:

I imply that the visions of nature are but a vision of the
motions of the divine imagination and that it is moving to a
complete mirroring of its own being, and when it attains

the perfect self-consciousness of itself the universe with-
draws into the Pralaya, as the eastern philosphers would
say. It would be true to say that the divine mind goes on
pilgrimage. (D., Ms. 441)

A.E. held that the "divine mind on pilgrimage" best
revealed itself through poets. But in "The Great Breath"
the cosmic intention is seriously obscured. Presumably
in the final stanza cosmic forces achieved a victory of
transcendence, but the images and rhythm suggest
exhaustion and weariness rather than a sense of divine
achievement. Here and elsewhere A.E. is guilty of many
imprecisions in his verse, in part because he attributed
to the psyche a control of verbal revelation surpassing
that of the critical mind.

"The Three Counsellors," also published in his first
collection, demonstrates A.E.'s use of Oriental sources.
In life and art, A.E. sought compromise; he tended to
reduce rather than to exploit oppositions. In this poem
a fairy "touched with dim and shadowy grace" the poet
during an inner struggle; it advised "quietness" and
disappeared. But a warrior's voice called to the poet,
"Awake"; prepare for battle but "Make of thy gentleness thy might." The poet asserts that a divine silence
may break the power of kings just as will may conquer
wantonness and mirth. The soul perceives the ultimate
wisdom needed by man:

> It was the wise all-seeing soul
> Who counselled neither war nor peace:
> "Only be thou thyself that goal
> In which the wars of time shall cease."

"Three Counsellors" began in a meditation on three
conflicting voices within an individual. A.E. said he had

been struggling with the meaning of the Bhagavad Gita
on Tamas, Rajas, and Satwa:

> Where the Gita makes Tamas sloth, I spiritualise this into
> Quietness, where the Gita spoke about action and the life
> of the warrior I transformed this into a sentence which ran
> as follows: "Make of thy gentleness thy might." For the
> Gita's conception of Satwa I substituted the purely
> subjective idea of not seeking in nature for war or peace,
> but that our own root nature should be our goal. (D. Ms.
> 443)

A.E. developed a faculty for "spiritualising" the harsh,
vulgar and brutal into pleas for quietness and gentleness.

A third poem, "The Well of All-Healing" stems from
A.E.'s search for a spiritual substratum in Irish folklore.
He heard of a woman in the west of Ireland who healed
people by fairy power: "There's a cure for all things in
the well at Ballykeele." These words lingered in A.E.'s
memory until they became a poem. Her words, A.E.
said, in *The Irish Theosophist* of September 15, 1897,
might be traced to a Druid source. This well, he
suggested, "is perhaps a humble starting-point for the
contemplation of . . . mighty mysteries."

> There's a cure for sorrow in the well at Ballylee
> Where the scarlet cressets hang over the trembling pool:

Through her healing powers, the countrywoman brings
peasants to the land of youth. Like Yeats, A.E.
expected symbols like the enchanted land and scarlet
berries to rekindle the spirit of the reader.

The three poems exhibit visionary, moralistic, and
folk elements of A.E.'s poems and partially answer the
charge that there is little variety in his poetry. Other

notable changes appear in his verse, many of them a result of the shift in his aspirations for Ireland over the years from 1890 to 1934. Yet A.E. tended to remain with his basic quatrain, developed probably from his acquaintance with Tennyson, Protestant hymns, and Edwin Arnold's *The Light of Asia.* Often in his later work A.E. uses a shorter line, some unrhymed verse, and more direct diction, and he does revise titles and phrasings in successive editions. From the first, however, A.E. describes his visions in what may have seemed to him a literal account of the event. At times the phrases are counters known only to the writer and an inner circle; he is said to have assigned precise meanings for the colors used in his poems. Significantly in depicting the quest of the soul, A.E. uses what might be called an esthetic of vagueness. He eschews precise physical details. In an exchange with W. B. Yeats about revisions of "Dana," A.E. wrote: "I mean to keep 'vast' and 'vague' as it exactly expresses my meaning, i.e., that mortals conceive of her as the Mother, as something too vast and indefinite to understand his nearness to the spirit" *(Letters of A.E. to W.B. Yeats,* p. 24). Vagueness seemed to him the proper mode for portraying the transcendent and sublime. Despite his belief in the correspondence between the earth world and the heaven world, A.E. curtails rather severely his description of man and nature. In poems like "The Symbol Seduces" he readily abandons the daily world for a permanent beauty, truth, and love.

A.E. hoped that *Song and Its Fountains* (1932) would serve as commentary on the provenance of his poems. He reexamines his early writing on the premise that poetry provides the best source for studying intuition and for showing consciousness at its peak. All poetry, he insists, sacred or secular, has its origins on the Mount of Transfiguration—

> and there is revelation in it and the mingling of heaven and earth. The Mount is a symbol for that peak of soul when, gone inward into itself, it draws nigh to its own divine root, and memory and imagination are shot through and through with the radiance of another nature. *(Song and Its Fountains,* p. 86)

A poem he felt to be also an oracle given to the waking consciousness from the psyche, which joins earth and heaven. The poet, A.E. said, must discover how his outer experiences are molded by his inner experiences; almost everything depends on one's aspirations, for they govern inspiration. Thus if the poet meditates on love, an oracle from the psyche may reveal some depths of divine love. From his early years he relied on the psyche; the purified psyche was a burning point through which the Infinite manifested itself as pure light through a prism. Yet as he developed his art, A.E. found that the outer mind grew to maturity slowly and at first lacked the facility to describe the discoveries of the psyche. He may be answering Yeats's charge that A.E. as a young man was at times incoherent.

A.E. also explained his poems by what he called his most profound line: "All my thoughts are throngs of living souls" ("Night"). At certain moments, the circle of his being intersected that of others, living and dead, at which time he was admitted to their inmost secrets. Thus a poet might speak with varied voices—according to his capacity to assimilate spirits of past or present.

Often these spirits illuminated his dreams. No psychology, he said, is so exciting as that which deals with the nightly return of the soul to the Absolute. Several poems and stories began in dreams; perhaps only A.E. would use the phrase, "as real as in dream."

Other poems issued from A.E.'s retrospective meditations, a means he developed to discover his spiritual life in previous incarnations. Through this form of meditation he retraced his life in Babylon and in Ireland at the time of the Druids. Like Yeats, A.E. carefully examined experiences that created guiding images. He learned that he was committed first to the search for beauty, then to the spirit of rebellion, and finally to a sense of selflessness. Later he learned that his calling was that of the mystical poet rather than the novelist. Indirectly in *Song and Its Fountains,* A.E. aligns himself with prophets and poets who bring ancient wisdom to modern man. For centuries, he said, revelations of beauty and spirit have come not from the churches "but from the poets who are still the seekers, and who at times have that lordly utterance as if the God was speaking through His prophets" (p. 91).

II

A.E.'s first volume of poems, *Homeward* (1894), is filled with the soft tones of twilight and dawn, of occasional diamond and white lights, of vast cycles of time, and rare moments of ecstasy. The poet struggles to apprehend the past glory of his soul and the perfection of the Great Breath or Brahma. Yet though the poet attains moments of mystical transport, his poems lack the definition of Vaughan's "I saw eternity the other night/ Like a great ring of light." A.E. moves toward the immeasurable in Oriental terms as in "Indian Song": "Shadow-petalled like the lotus, . . .," generally evoking a world-weariness. He tries to create a sense of immense spiritual powers, remote, sparkling, and ineffable, to cast a spell over men and lure them to their home in the Absolute.

A.E. explores in the poems some of the dilemmas attached to the vocation of mystical poet. In their early work, both A.E. and Yeats seem preoccupied with the pattern set by King Fergus, i.e., a king, a man of action, leaves court and battlefield to become a Druid, a man of contemplation; he then discovers the loneliness of his exile from mankind and divinity. A.E.'s "To One Consecrated" describes the mixed joy and suffering that are the lot of the visionary. The poet feels that he is nourished by the Mighty Mother, the earth, who grants him love and gentleness but at a price: "a crown of thorns." When other men look at the consecrated one, they fail to see the ring of wounding spears on his head.

The consecrated one develops defenses; he must protect himself from "The might that shaped itself through storm and stress/ In chaos" ("Echoes"). His insight is founded on a sacramental perception; he trains himself to see the immortal in the mortal, climbing a Platonic ladder: "Through loved things rising up to Love's own ways . . ." ("Symbolism"). While A.E. subscribed to the symbolism based on the correspondence between the heaven world and the earth world, he spurned the symbolism of Arthur Symons, calling it sensual and decadent. Yet A.E. had difficulty in describing the top rungs of the Platonic ladder, often resorting to brief, direct passages, such as: "White, for Thy whiteness all desires burn./ And, with what longing once again I turn!" ("Desire").

A series of four poems contains some of his best work in *Homeward*—"Dusk," "Night," "Dawn," and "Day." These brief poems depict stages in man's spiritual journey, as if A.E. were an impressionist viewing the same object under varying light. In "Dusk," smoke breaks the line of sky in a village. Apparently smoke serves as the imagination or Yeats's wind among the reeds to join earth and sky, matter and spirit. "Night" is the time for union with the Absolute and rapture, "alone in primal ecstasy." "Dawn" contains the "Moment that holds all moments," but it marks the speaker's return to the prosaic world, his fire separated from that of divinity. "Day" asserts that an iron will keeps man out of the heaven world, yet the path is not entirely blocked, for each dream is a burning glass "where through to darkness from the Light of Lights/ Its rays in splendour pass." In these poems A.E. compresses the ancient wisdom on the exile of the soul from divinity and its quest for a final home.

In a review of *Homeward,* W. B. Yeats quoted "Truth" in full as well as "Sung on a By-Way" and "Our Thrones Decay." Perhaps the most effective poem, however, is "Dust," in which the poet claims that ordinary earth "Is thrilled with fire of hidden day,/ And haunted by all mystery." Yeats also singled out several lines from other poems for quotation. After regretting awkward phrasings and cadences, Yeats said, "but taken all in all, it is the most haunting book I have seen these many days." He called A.E. the "arch-visionary" of the Theosophical Household and praised the pathos of the book.

The Earth Breath (1897) overflows with A.E.'s devotion to his patroness, the Earth Mother. He seems to discover the earth anew in poems like "A New World": "And all I thought of heaven before/ I find in earth below." He concludes: "And with the earth my heart is glad." But A.E. exalts the principle of earth rather than particular objects, persons, or events. Also his new enthusiasm is not pervasive enough to resolve the old conflicts of the consecrated one. A boy, for instance, discovers his visionary powers only to learn that "a life of tears, tears/ He had won for himself that day" ("Awakening"). "A New Theme" acknowledges the difficulty of reaching the heights of mysticism: "I strive to blow the magic horn;/ It feebly murmureth." Had he the power to sound the horn, he would arouse every exile to search for his spiritual homeland.

"The Message of St. John" and "The Fountain of Shadowy Beauty," both long poems, reflect A.E.'s ambition to become a significant mystical poet. In the latter poem a visionary finds a crystal boat and a pilot to lead him to his "brother-self" in a resplendent fountain, presumably an exalted state of mysticism or the source of cosmic creation. Occasionally A.E. hits upon a vivid metaphor to emphasize the gulf between the two worlds that contend for man's passion. A notable one from "Immortality" reads: "We must pass like smoke or live within the spirit's fire." In contemplating a figure of Janus, the poet dwells on the mystery of how we go through one door to life, and another to death, impelled by spirit or sense. Janus also suggests to the poet the thin veil separating hell and paradise.

The conflicts within the visionary are further developed in poems on the theme of sacrifice. A.E. returns to this theme through the years as if it were a painful burden that cannot be shed with finality. The protagonist of "Love" claims that if he were resting in the Absolute, "I would still hear the cry of the fallen recalling me back from above,/ To go down to the side of the people who weep in the shadow of death." Yet the poet derives a compensation for the soul serving those enslaved spirits on earth. The soul's earthly struggles provide it with a higher knowledge than the angels have. "The Man and the Angel," one of A.E.'s best poems, claims that man's wisdom has a richness the angels lack, for man's knowledge is gained through suffering and purification of mortal experience, whereas the angels are restricted to knowledge based on pure intuition. At this stage the poet accepts conflict of head and heart as inevitable, a part of the sacrifice the visionary must make in his present incarnation. In "Duality" the poet is torn between the demands of his "ruby heart" and those of "a pure cold spirit." He praises the heart, saying that even God pities the heart because it contends with deathless powers; such conflicts are essential to human life.

Published when he was thirty-seven years old, *The Divine Vision* (1904) contains numerous allusions to Celtic gods and heroes, although A.E. first used Irish references as early as 1895. With his assimilation of Irish material, A.E. instills a new energy in many quatrains. The protagonist of "A Farewell" is "fired by a Danaan whisper of battles afar in the world" to return as master and to fight like "the bright Hound of Ulla" "to conquer the heavens and battle for kingship on high." A.E. breaks the dreamy atmosphere of his poems with references to the waves of Toth, Rury, and Cleena: "The three great waves leap up exulting in their joy,/ Remembering the past, the immemorial deeds/ The Danaan gods had wrought in guise of mortal men, . . ." Some of his Irish poems like "The Twilight of the Earth" would be confusing without A.E.'s notes. The following lines refer to the end of a cosmic cycle: "The Sacred Hazels' blooms are shed,/ The Nuts of knowledge harvested." The hazel is the Celtic tree of life, the nuts of knowledge the source of inspiration and wisdom. Nuts drop in Connla's well, an equivalent to the first fountain of mysticism.

Several poems in *The Divine Vision* point to a new conflict within A.E.'s protagonists—the poet seeks both human and divine love, but for him one type of love excludes the other. For instance, in "Love from Afar," the speaker encounters a burning fire and calls out, "Spirit, I love you." Immediately he sees fading around him "the dim unreal land of day." Regarding love, the oracles from the psyche are often in conflict: "The wisdom before which love grew chill would be opposed by oracles speaking of an immortality of love" (*Song and Its Fountains*, p. 54). While Yeats vacillated between psyche and the beloved, A.E. has spiritual love prevail without question. "The Message" opposes spirit to Cupid. A flame of love is sent to the beloved, but a divinity will save her from the arrows of Cupid and from the fiery birds of Angus that bring love or death. But the divine intention is clear: "I give you the star-fire, the heart-way to Paradise,/ With no death after, no arrow with stinging pains." "The Vision of Love" depicts a transcendent passion. At twilight the eyes of the beloved are like "burnished stones"; momentarily the lovers "love in infinite spaces, forgetting . . . the lips so near," but a wind draws the poet back to the fallen world. In his divine passion the visionary perceives ancient love in "The hearts of men" ("The Parting of the Ways"). A.E. holds spiritual love as the highest value for men; it belongs neither to youth nor age, but its beauty and permanence make human wisdom and truth seem empty ("The Grey Eros").

In "Poems 1903-1920," a section of *Selected Poems*, A.E. applies his cosmic teachings to world and personal crises, but he excluded from this section most of his poems on World War I, published in *Gods of War* (1915). Probably A.E. considered his anti-war poems too strident for the reflective atmosphere of *Selected Poems*. Still he spoke openly to the Irish in exhortation or indignation on many occasions. "An Irish Face" examines the impact of ancestral memories on a modern Irish girl. Her face reflects the stories of Deirdre, Cuchulain, Ferdiad, and the Wild Geese. The Irish could become a lordlier race, he feels, if they would contemplate the heroism and sorrow in their myths. A.E. attacks the smugness of the Irish in his apologia, "On Behalf of Some Irishmen not Followers of Tradition," a widely anthologized poem with many forceful lines. The poet defends the Anglo-Irish, artists, and probably Theosophists from the attack of the majority of

Irishmen, Christians who worship at an extinct fire and destroy their individuality by a preoccupation with pain and suffering:

> The worship of the dead is not
> A worship that our hearts allow
> Though every famous shade were wrought
> With woven thorns above the brow.

The poet allies himself with a nation not yet born, the Ireland of the heart and spirit. He looks for his spiritual country in the future: "our lips would gladlier hail/ The firstborn of the Coming Race/ Than the last splendour of the Gael." Against the sceptred myth of Christianity he proclaims "The golden heresy of truth," the goal for a rebel trying to create a new race of men.

Despite the atrocities of World War I, A.E. often retained a cosmic detachment. "Continuity" holds that empires pass away but flowers and stars remain. Whatever the catastrophe, "The Everlasting works Its will." Despite the destruction, "Though the crushed jewels droop and fade/ The Artist's labours will not cease. . . ."

A.E.'s first volume in twenty-one years, *Voices of the Stones*, contains several of the poet's personal reactions as a lifetime believer in theosophical principles; he comments on the bond between the poet and his principles, on the wisdom that grows out of the years of viewing life in theosophical terms. In his later search for mystical experience, A.E. becomes increasingly aware of his own physical decline, the birth of a "terrible beauty" in Ireland, the barbarism of World War I, the destruction of his cooperative creameries by the Black and Tans, and the erosion of his dream for a spiritual renaissance.

A.E. builds a defense against the chaos of age and the era by strengthening the will. In comments on the poetic process he values will more highly than imagination. As early as his first volume of poems, A.E. deplored the decay of will in modern man: "For a dream-shaft pierced it through/ From the Unknown Archer's bow" ("Sung on a By-Way"). At present man's will is misguided or paralyzed; most men have no knowledge of the methods of directing their will toward mystical heights. "Waste" does not allude to the horrors and tragedy of war; rather the poet claims that suffering and pain are wasted if man does not pursue beauty. Men die in vain if they have no exalted images within; such a death he calls a sin against the Holy Ghost. "Watchers" adds that modern men have become brutes, losing their kinship with Elohim, his term for the shining ones. In a rare use of the grotesque, A.E. describes the demonic forces in the world: "kestrel, snake and rat . . . / Glaring through eyeholes that let in no light." One of his few sonnets. "Watchers," is his severest indictment of modern civilization.

Despite the general failure of will, A.E. praises an heroic exception in "A Prisoner." Terence MacSwiney, Lord Mayor of Cork, died after a seventy-four day hunger strike in Brixton Prison in September 1920. The first lines suggest the desperate resolution of MacSwiney: "See, though the oil be low, more purely still and higher/ The flame burns in the body's lamp." But in a large part of the poem, the poet exhorts the readers to emulate MacSwiney's Promethean will and its lonely conquest.

The long poem "Michael" is undergirded with A.E.'s hope for a revival of heroic will in Ireland, as well as a concern with images that may bring about a renewal of will. A.E. awoke one morning to find some verses "tumbled out of the dream state into the waking." An odd line appeared, unrelated to the rest of the poem. Sensing that the poem "had been completed in dream," A.E. walked about the hills until the poem was finished, the odd line falling into a passage on the will discovering its proper goal in a dream (*Song and Its Fountains*, pp. 58, 59). Much admired by J. B. Yeats, "Michael" tells the story of a Donegal youth who finds the Gaelic past, offers himself to the Volunteers, and dies in the insurrection of 1916. When he worked in a warehouse in Dublin, Michael discovered his "spiritual heritage,/ The story from the gods that ran/ Through many a cycle down to man." Michael learns of Cuchulain, the Fianna, and the Irish patriots of the nineteenth century. Soon his individual self merges with that of the race, and Michael transcends the Donegal farmer and the Dublin warehouseman because the heroic Irish past has given meaning to his life and death.

With *Vale* (1931) A.E. seems to bid farewell to life and poetry. He may have feared a poetic dryness in his last years, or he may have regarded these poems as his final expression of spirit in a world more and more dominated by scientific naturalism. In "The Farewell of Pan," a theosophical fantasy, Pan presides over a last supper with "sweet apostles" bending their brows, the table spread with stars, the bread of earth, and the holy wine of air. But A.E.'s Pan lacks the sprightliness of James Stephens' character in *The Crock of Gold*; rather he speaks with the voice of A.E.'s consecrated one:

> We long for the day
> When this shadow show shall be over, the masks we wore
>   thrown away—
> The monstrous masks that veiled us, of satyr, demon and
>   faun—
> And be lovely, starry and ancient with youth as we were
>   in the dawn.

Throughout his work A.E. attends only in passing to the masks of satyr, demon, and faun, but curiously he confesses in *Song and Its Fountains* that he was too often in league with satyr and faun for the best impulses of spirit to rule him (p. 8).

A.E. frequently examines the role of guiding images in the psyche; he searches for the seeds that make a man a hero, mystic, or traitor. W. B. Yeats, A.E. said, was dominated by the myth of duality of the self, of being and shadow. A.E.'s "Germinal," one of his best known poems, cites Dante, Caesar, and Judas as examples of men who hear or neglect the call of spirit in youth: "In the lost boyhood of Judas/ Christ was betrayed." A.E.'s own guiding myth was that of the starry child, the soul as visionary. In age, he wished he had invited the sage instead of the starry child, for the sage would have changed that which had been harsh in youth to something pleasant in later years. A.E. however, does not elaborate on this transformation, but he returns to the theme that our aspirations become our inspiration: "Our prayers are answered, oh to be wise in prayers."

A.E.'s nostalgia for the Household emerges in "How?" with its gracious tribute to his old friends, Mrs.

Dick and James Pryse. In an uncharacteristic bit of
sentimentality A.E. states that his life has been in vain if
he does not find the friends of the Household in
eternity just as they were in his youth. A more
significant expression of his spiritual themes fills "Dark
Weeping," an ode first published in an illustrated
booklet. This poem traces the history of the soul,
stressing the body's complaint against the soul and the
soul's complaint against the earth-world. The speaker
asks why dreams bring sadness to body and soul: "The
proud and plumed will" often wounds an innocent
party, the body. In dreams, will learns of tyrannical
foes; it encounters "a firmament ablaze/ With high,
angered, burning, immortal faces." Yet the poet cele-
brates the release of creative powers in dreams and
quotes Vedic seers who speak of the power of the soul
in sleep to construct cities, lamps, or carnivals for
whirling dryads. He awakes "with a pillow wet with
dreams" because the soul anticipates that halfway
between heaven and earth it will lose memory of its
divinity. Soul dreads life on earth where it becomes a
slave, where its own beauty is spurned as a fiction,
where its sacrifices are discounted as dreams, and where
"obscene hunters" mock tales of its nobility. "Dark
Weeping," a late expression of A.E.'s cosmic views, has
a disturbing emphasis on the sadness of both body and
soul.

Surprisingly, A.E. includes two long poems in *The
House of the Titans* (1934), one on the Dark Lady of
Shakespeare's sonnets and the other on his cosmic
system fitted to a Celtic myth. This late harvest may be
accounted for in part by his new leisure, his continuing

ambition to express the essence of his visions of the 1890s, and his disillusionment with what he called the crazy Gaeldom of the Irish Free State.

In "The Dark Lady" A.E. applies his theory of *anima mundi* to a frequent topic of Dublin literary discussion—solving the riddle of Shakespeare's life and work. In the library scene of *Ulysses* Stephen Dedalus advances his theory, a theory to which A.E. objected on the grounds that it is improper to explain literary work through the author's biography. "The Dark Lady" makes a belated response to a discussion that had been fed by the work of Sidney Lee, Frank Harris, Georg Brandes, and the progenitor of biographical theories, Edward Dowden. In 1934 A.E. wrote that he had been imagining what kind of woman Shakespeare loved; he had a dream in which he was "near in spirit to the Dark Lady who was breathing profound profundities of passion into my spirit, all about her traffic with the poet." A.E. added, "My idea is that Shakespeare was in half-conscious internal contact with other souls". (D. Ms. 631). Writers like Balzac and Shakespeare thought they were working by art or imagination but they were actually filled with spirits they had not known in life; these spirits were real and "revealed more of themselves in that profundity of being than if they had met and spoken day by day where the truth of life hides itself under many disguises" (*Song and Its Fountains,* p. 42).

In "The Dark Lady," a long soliloquy in blank verse, there is no dramatic situation or an implied audience as in Browning's monologues. Neither does the dark lady attain the intensity of passion suggested by her torment and determination. The poem, however, exemplifies

A.E.'s view of the poetic process. Like a completed soul in A.E.'s cosmology, the dark lady sacrifices herself to rescue Shakespeare from a homosexual relationship with the Friend, "so airy ivory of limb." To keep the Friend away from Shakespeare, she seduces the Friend but then discovers herself loving contrary types: "one godlike in mind/ And one the outer image of the mind." Torn between these desires, the dark lady does not know whether she is driven by god or devil, by sexual love for the Friend or by spiritual love for Shakespeare. She fails to save Shakespeare from "an unnatural love,/ The kind that marred the Grecian genius." But her spirit lives within Shakespeare's imagination. Although Shakespeare dismisses her without a word, she recognizes his forgiveness in *The Tempest,* for she imagined herself "a maid/ Bred on a fairy isle who knew not man" and Shakespeare was "an enchanter with spirits at his command/ And they had loved each other."

"The House of the Titans," A.E.'s most ambitious poem, equals in length about two books of *Paradise Lost,* and it might be called a brief epic. In the first half of the poem King Nuada, ruler of the fallen Titans who are groveling on the floor of a large hall, describes the Celtic cosmogony much as A.E. summarized it in *The Candle of Vision.* The second half of the poem contains speeches by an avatar similar to the one A.E. dreamed of in the 1890s. Here he is called the Master of Many Arts and appears on a winged horse with a sunrise blazing behind him. He is a manifestation of Lugh, the sun god. The Master of Many Arts seeks admission to the Titans to restore them to wholeness, i.e., to complete their souls, but he is rejected by King Nuada.

The Master of Many Arts appears in turn as an enchanter, a poet, a prophet, and a healer, but under each mask he is refused because King Nuada insists that he has an equivalent skill among the Titans. Finally the Master of Many Arts overcomes King Nuada by explaining the law of sacrifice and the primacy of will. Although the poem has little action and long expository passages, it provides remarkable evidence of A.E.'s persistence in seeking new Irish forms for presenting his basic beliefs.

A.E.'s reputation as poet reached its zenith in the praise given him in Ernest Boyd's *Ireland's Literary Renaissance* (1916 and 1922). It may have reached its nadir in Eric Bentley's remark that a reading of A.E. and Edward Martyn would convince anyone that an Irish Renaissance never existed (*The Permanence of Yeats*, p. 237). But if one considers his forty years as a mystical poet, it can be said that A.E. felt confident he was carrying out the essential task of the artist: "... it is through the poets and musicians that we can get the sense of a glory transmitted from another nature, and as we mingle our imagination with theirs we are exalted and have the heartache of infinite desire" (*Song and Its Fountains*, p. 91).

POSTSCRIPT: A.E. AS PUBLISHER

As this book goes to press still another aspect of A.E. is discovered, that of publisher, "my first attempt at book production," as he writes in his short preface. The book is a pamphlet of twenty pages, limited to 50 numbered copies signed in red initials. It has variant titles: NINE / WHISTLER / LETTERS on the brown paper cover and half-title, but on the title page, NINE LETTERS / TO / TH. WATTS-DUNTON / FROM / J. McN. WHISTLER. At the foot is a diamond with the initials inset, followed by CHELSEA MCMXXII, a layout repeated at the end of the preface. Five of the letters can be dated by postmarks (1878, 1885, 1888, 1889); they were loaned by Mr. T. J. Wise. The emblem on the inside of the rear end-paper indicates that the booklet was published by the Chiswick Press. The book was given to R. M. Kain by John L. Folts, Jr. of March, Milligan & Company, Bethesda, Maryland.

Selected Bibliography

Alan Denson has compiled with a meticulous care a complete list of A.E.'s writings and paintings in:
Printed Writings by George W. Russell (AE): A Bibliography. Evanston, Ill. Northwestern University Press, 1961.
Corrections and additional items are included in the following work by Mr. Denson:
James H. Cousins (1873-1956) and Margaret E. Cousins (1878-1954), a Bio Bibliographical Survey. Kendal, England: Alan Denson, 1967.
A six-volume edition of the collected works of A.E., edited by Henry Summerfield. Forthcoming.

WORKS BY A.E.

The Avatars: A Futurist Fantasy. London and New York: Macmillan and Co., 1933.

The Candle of Vision. London: Macmillan and Co., 1918.

Collected Poems. London: Macmillan and Co., 1913, 1919, 1926, 1935.

The Divine Vision and Other Poems. London and New York: The Macmillan Co., 1904.

The Earth Breath and Other Poems. London: John Lane, 1897.

Homeward: Songs by the Way. Dublin: Whaley, 1894.

The House of the Titans and Other Poems. London and New York: The Macmillan Co., 1934.

Imaginations and Reveries. Dublin and London: Maunsel, 1915.

The Interpreters. London: Macmillan and Co., 1922.

Letters from AE, edited by Alan Denson. London: Abelard and Schuman, 1961.

The Living Torch, edited by Monk Gibbon. London: The Macmillan Co., 1937.

The National Being: Some Thoughts on Irish Polity. Dublin and London: Maunsel and Co., 1916.

Selected Poems. London and New York: Macmillan and Co., 1935. (Golden Treasury Series, 1951.)

Song and Its Fountains. London and New York: The Macmillan Co., 1932.

Vale and Other Poems. London and New York: The Macmillan Co., 1931.

Voices of the Stones. London and New York: The Macmillan Co., 1925.

PAMPHLETS

Cooperation and Nationality. Dublin: Maunsel and Co., 1912.

The Future of Ireland and the Awakening of the Fires. Dublin: n.p., 1897.

Ideals in Ireland: Priest or Hero? Dublin: n.p., 1897.

The Inner and Outer Ireland. Dublin: Talbot Press, 1921.

The Renewal of Youth. London: The Orpheus Press, 1911.

Some Irish Essays. Dublin: Maunsel and Co., 1906.

Some Passages from the Letters of A.E. to W. B. Yeats. Dublin: Cuala Press, 1936.

Twenty-Five Years of Irish Nationalism. New York: Council on Foreign Affairs, 1929, originally in *Foreign Affairs* 7, (January 1929): 204-20.

CRITICAL STUDIES

Boyd, Ernest A. *Ireland's Literary Renaissance*. New York: John Lane, 1916. Rev. ed. New York: A. A. Knopf, 1922.

Curran, Constantine. "George Russell, (AE), 1867-1935." *Studies* 24 (September 1935): 366-78.

Daniels, William. "AE: 1867-1967." *Irish University Review* 4 (Spring 1967): 107-20.

Denson, Alan. *G. W. Russell (AE): A Centennial Assessment.* Kendal, England: Alan Denson, 1968.

Figgis, Darrell. *A.E. (George W. Russell), A Study of a Man and a Nation.* Dublin: Maunsel, 1916.

Gibbon, Monk. "AE, The Years of Mystery." *The Dublin Magazine* (January-March 1956): pp. 8-21.

　　　"Childhood and Early Youth of A.E." *The Dublin Magazine* (April-June 1955) pp. 6-14, and (July-September 1955) pp. 8-17.

Howarth, Herbert. *The Irish Writers 1880-1940: Literature Under Parnell's Star.* New York: Hill and Wang, 1958.

Jenkins, Ralph. "Theosophy in Scylla and Charybdis." *Modern Fiction Studies* (Spring 1969), pp. 35-48.

Magee, William (pseud. John Eglinton). *A Memoir of A.E.* London: Macmillan, 1937.

Moore, George. *Hail and Farewell*, comprising *Ave* (1911), *Salve* (1912), and *Vale* (1914). London: Heinemann.

Nevin, Donal, ed. *1913: Jim Larkin and the Dublin Lock-out.* Dublin: Workers' Union of Ireland, 1964. A collection of documents, including statements by A.E., James Connolly, Constance Markievicz, Maud Gonne McBride, O'Casey, Pearse, Stephens, and Yeats.

Summerfield, Henry. "A Mystic in the Modern World." *Iliff Review* 26 (1969): 13-21.

———. *That Myriad-Minded Man: A Biography of G. W. Russell (A.E.).* Forthcoming.